The *Real*

McCoy

Al McCoy

With Rich Wolfe

Layout: The Printed Page, Phoenix, AZ
Author's agent: T. Roy Gaul

Rich Wolfe can be reached at 602-738-5889

ISBN: 978-0-9800978-7-0

Printed in the United States

*__PAGE TWO.__ In 1941, the news director at a small radio station in Kalamazoo, Michigan hired Harry Caray who had been employed at a station in Joliet, Illinois. The news director's name was Paul Harvey. Yes, that PAUL HARVEY! "And now, you know the rest of the story…"

DEDICATION

To my #1 Team: my family
My wife, Georgia
and sons Michael, Jay and Jerry
~Al McCoy

To the Original Sun: Dick Van Arsdale
Fun to watch play, fun to be with,
just a super guy and friend for 42 years

~Rich Wolfe

All of Al McCoy's proceeds from this book
will be donated to his hometown public library
in Williams, Iowa and to Phoenix Suns Charities.

ACKNOWLEDGMENTS

During the making of this book the co-author, Rich Wolfe, suffered a debilitating neck, spine, and head injury that required several months of hospitalization. Stepping up to do the editing in his absence were the ever helpful Tom Ambrose of the Phoenix Suns; Mark Bast of Grand Rapids, Michigan; and prolific author and retired Indiana Pacers big shot Dale Ratermann.

Thanks to a couple of wonder women who have been indispensable sidekicks for many years and helped make this book a reality—Ellen Brewer in Edmond, Oklahoma, and Lisa Liddy at The Printed Page in Phoenix.

Also a tip of the hat to Tucker Wolfe of Phoenix and Gene Cervelli of Paradise Valley, Arizona.

CONTENTS

Chapter 1

SWEET HOME IOWA

How'ya Gonna Keep 'Em Down on the Farm After They've Seen Des Moines

I grew up in Williams, Iowa: population 600. There were around 100 kids in the high school. I lived on a farm two-and-a-half miles from town. We played some type of sport every day, winter or summer. I'd ride my bike into town, or I'd run the two-and-a-half miles, because I was in good shape. Sometimes I rode the school bus to school, and coming home, the driver would let me off a mile from home, and I'd make the rest of the trip on foot. When we played baseball, we'd start off with **TENNIS*** balls, because we could throw curves with them. Sports were a big part of my everyday life, even though I lived on a farm.

I heard all the depression stories about the farmers not being able to sell corn so they used it for heat in the winter instead of coal. That really happened when we lived on the farm.

When I was four years old, we moved to a farm about two-and-a-half miles west of Williams, Iowa. It was a 200-acre farm which my dad was renting. He eventually, through the years, was able to purchase the farm, which was owned by the Metropolitan Life Insurance Company. A lot of big companies bought farms during the depression and made a lot of money when they sold them. I know it took a lot of hard work for my dad to eventually become the owner of that farm. It was a big day for us when it happened.

When we moved, we had no electricity, no running water...but I never really heard anybody complain about it. We knew that people who lived in towns had those things. I guess the farmers felt that eventually they would get those things, too.

We had air conditioning—we opened a window in our bedroom in July and August! We didn't even know about air conditioning.

---

*In what sport was Chris Evert the leading money winner in 1974? The answer: Horse Racing. The owner, Carl Rosen, named his horses after **TENNIS** players. The horse named Chris Evert won $551,063 with five wins in eight starts.

We loved that hot, humid weather in July and August because that was supposed to make the corn grow so we looked forward to that.

We finally did get electricity because we were able to get that big floor-model radio when I was about eight so we had to have gotten it by then. When we did get electricity and running water, we felt we were just like everybody else.

My mother and father took me to the Iowa State Fair in Des Moines when I was eight years old. The State Fair in Iowa is a pretty big deal. As an eight-year-old, I am walking around, and I see up ahead that there is a booth from one of the local radio stations in Des Moines. It happened to be KRNT. One of the radio personalities was standing out in front doing a "man on the street" live broadcast. As I was approaching, I could see that he was stopping people and asking them questions. As I got closer, the radio personality saw me, walked over to me with a microphone in hand, and said, "We have a young fellow here. Son, what do you think about the Iowa State Fair?" I reached up and took the microphone from him and went into a disc jockey routine, saying, "We're here at the Iowa State Fair...and let's talk about hits and our hit parade!" I went on and on, naming radio songs that were on the hit parade . This radio personality finally reached out and took the microphone from me and said, "Well, I guess I know who is going to be replacing me here in a few years!" That was my first time on live radio, and it was an unforgettable moment.

As kids, we used to do a lot of things by ourselves. You could throw a ball up on the roof of the barn, watch it roll down, and catch it. I had a basketball hoop up on a tree. You had to be careful if you drove in too hard, though. My school buddies played something every single day. When I got into high school and was on the basketball team, for some reason, we didn't think the coach would let us use the gym on Saturdays. On a Saturday, I got together with two of the players on our team, two brothers who also lived on a farm not far from me. We went over to the gym and climbed up to one of the very high windows and got into the gym. This became a regular thing. One day, the coach comes down, and he was all upset, asking "What are you doing in here? How did you get in?" We hemmed and hawed around. He said, "Well, why didn't you tell me? I'll open the gym for you any day or night you want to come down and play." We hadn't thought he would go along with it, but that was how bad some of us wanted to play.

We'd play baseball, basketball, whatever was in season. I was fortunate enough to make the team in my sophomore year in high school. We had a new coach come in my freshman year, Chuck Lovin, who had just gotten out of the service and took over the coaching reins at Williams High School. He ran a tough ship—no question about it. We had some great teams. I was able to start in my sophomore year. In fact, Dick Knickerbocker and I were the starting guards most of the time our sophomore, junior and senior years. Our junior and senior years, we had real good teams. My coach still likes to tell the story about when people would ask him, "How come Al McCoy gets so much playing time?" Coach Lovin would tell them, "Well, when he's not in the game, he's on the bench sitting next to me. He's pretending that he's broadcasting the game. He's so bad I can't stand it...so I just send him back in the game." He was kidding, of course, because he did like me as a player, and we still have a great relationship. He taught me that it's a lot more fun to win than it is to lose. As I mentioned, we had some good teams. My senior year, we won 16 games in a row, but then didn't have very good luck come tournament time. We had better luck at tournament time my junior year.

My junior and senior years in high school I got involved in speech contests. I don't even know if they still have these anymore. My junior year, I got a Division I rating in radio speaking. You couldn't do the same one the next year so I did extemporaneous speaking and got a Division I there. That was really responsible for me getting a partial scholarship to attend Drake University, which I did after I graduated from high school. My graduating class from Williams High School had 15 students.

Drake did not have a radio or a broadcasting major at Drake University so I became a drama/speech major and minored in broadcast journalism. I took all the radio classes that were offered. Two professors certainly were very instrumental during my days at Drake University. James Fiderlick was the head of the Drama Department. He was an unbelievable person. Going to his classes was almost like going to church. He not only taught drama and speech, he taught you a way of life. He had come out of Yale, and he was a wonderful, wonderful man. The professor who became a real mentor was the head of the radio department, Jim Duncan. He was a brilliant individual. He'd been named one of the 'top 50' professors by Esquire Magazine. He had a strong affiliation with Drake University. It was interesting because our relationship really became strong my first year.

I asked him if I could borrow a recorder and tape one of the Drake University basketball games. He told me "Don't rush into things. We usually don't let students do this until they get into their junior or senior year. You have a lot of time to do something like that." I just kept bugging him about it, and finally one Friday morning in class, he said, "Okay, I'll let you check out a recorder, and I'll make a call for you to get a place at the Drake game on Saturday night. You can go down and try your luck."

I have to tell you it was a wire recorder. Anybody ever hear about wire recorders? Well, this was one. I took it and got my place up in the press box area, where I recorded this great basketball game. The next week I took it in to class and gave him back the recorder and said, "I hope you'll have an opportunity to critique it." He said, "Okay, okay." A week went by...two weeks went by, and I would bring it up. He'd say, "Oh, I'll get to it one of these days." Finally, after several weeks had passed, one day I came into class as he walked out of his office, which was right by the classroom. He said, "Al McCoy, come into my office." I thought, "Oh boy. What did I do now?" I went into his office, shut the door and walked over to him. He was, "How long have you been broadcasting basketball?" I said, "Well, I don't know." He said, "I listened to your recording. You do a better job than anyone who is working professionally in this city right now." From that point on, we developed a close relationship. He was so instrumental in preparing me for the real world of broadcasting. The track where the Drake Relays is held is named after Jim Duncan. He was the announcer for the Drake Relays for years.

I think one of the high points, early in my career, was when Professor Duncan retired, and he was told he could invite three people to speak at his retirement. The three people he selected were the president of the University at the time, Dolph Pulliam, who had played basketball at Drake University when Drake went to the Final Four, and me. That was a tremendous honor for me to speak at his retirement. Jim Duncan was an individual who was a very, very huge part of any success I have been able to attain in broadcasting.

At the end of my freshman year at Drake, I decided the broadcast world was ready for me. I sent out 25 audition tapes to stations in the Midwest. I got one reply. Believe it or not, it was from KJFJ, Webster City, Iowa, the town that was just 15 miles from my home town. I went up—it was about 50 miles from Des Moines and did another audition there. They had an announcer who had been drafted. I got the job and started working there at the tail end of the school year, in May. I worked there all summer. It was a big opportunity for me because I did everything. I was a disc jockey and did some news. We were fortunate enough to do some baseball because there was an excellent semi-pro league in Iowa and Minnesota in those days. The station was owned by the newspaper in Webster City, Iowa, *The Daily Freeman Journal.* The sports editor of the newspaper and I broadcast the weekend semi-pro baseball games. That was a terrific experience for me there. I thought very seriously about not returning to Drake. I felt I didn't need any more education. Finally I decided I would go back and I continued to work weekends for a while at KJFJ, while I was attending Drake my sophomore year.

Then, an amazing thing happened. The big station in the Midwest in those days was WHO in Des Moines, a 50,000 watt, Clear

Channel, and they had just gotten FM. They came to Professor Duncan at Drake to see if there was anyone who could do a show on FM and do some other announcing on their staff. During this period of time, in the 50's when I was at Drake, there were a lot of older students, fellows who had been in the service and had come back to college on the GI bill. Many of those who were in the radio classes had actually worked in radio and gone into the service and now were back in school. Four of us were selected to audition for the job. WHO was an NBC station, and they gave us the NBC Network radio audition. It was unbelievable—all these foreign names, classical music and composers. When I did that audition, I was perspiring—I was a nervous wreck. I didn't get the job. Another individual was hired for that job. He started around the first of December. As things do happen, during Christmas vacation, I was home with my parents and got a call from Professor Jim Duncan telling me to call the program director at WHO right away because the guy they had hired didn't work out. I was number two on their list, an they wanted to talk to me. So, I got the job at WHO.

At first, at WHO, I had that schedule and then the station went all-night for the first time. I had a chance to work on the all-night show and that was terrific for me to be working at a 50,000 watt clear channel station.

When I had been there a year, one afternoon, the gentleman who I reported to, and who had been responsible for hiring me, came down to the studio when I was on the air. He said, quite frankly, and I don't think I've ever told this story to anybody before, "Al, you know, we really like you here. You're a favorite of our people, but I don't think you really have a real future in being on the air." I was a little stunned...to say the least. He said, "You know, there are a lot of other things you can do in broadcasting—there's production, sales, promotion. I just don't think you have what it's going to take to be real successful as an on-the-air personality." I don't have to tell you that this was a shock. My bubble was burst! He said, "We want you to stay on here. We want you to continue to work, but I'm going to take you off this show. I'd like to have you work in our production department. We'll still use you, in some instances, on the air, but not as much, and I'd like to see you get into some other areas of broadcasting because I just don't think you're going to be successful long-term as an on-the-air person."

I knew this was probably the biggest decision I was ever going to have to make in my life. I could have just rolled over and said, "he's correct," and that's the way it's going to be. But, that night, I had a dance job. I wasn't thinking too much about playing with the band that night...I was thinking about what he had told me. Sometime that night, I made a decision. I don't care what he says. I don't think he's right. I think I am going to be able to do what I want to do. Becoming a play-by-play sportscaster was really what I had set my goal for, definitely. I said, "Well, he may think I don't have it...I still think I do."

It was interesting that a short time after that, I made a trip back down to KJFJ in Webster City to see some of the people. I saw the manager, who had been great to me when I was working there. I told him the story, and he said, "Hey, what do they know? Don't believe what one guy is going to tell you." I stayed at WHO in the production department and doing some limited air work for a while, but at the same time I started looking around.

I had done some work for a gentleman who had has since become a lifelong friend, Jim Zabel, who was the voice of the University of Iowa football and basketball forever and who still does a Sunday night show on WHO from his home in Scottsdale. I've known Jim all those years and he's become a very, very good friend and probably the best known radio-television personality ever in the state of Iowa. I did some work with him during that period. I realized I was never going to take his job because he had been there many, many years, and would be there many more.

There was another station in Des Moines, KWDM, a small family-owned station, owned by the Weber family. I remember when they went on the air and their call letters were 'Keep Watching

Des Moines.' They hired some students as part-time people. They hired me. When I went back and resigned at WHO, people could not believe it. They said, "Oh, how can anyone leave WHO, the biggest station in the Midwest?"

I did because I wanted to do what I wanted to do. KWDM did all kinds of play-by-play. They did high school. They did college. I fit in very, very well. The Weber family was terrific to me. I mentioned two of the fellows that were there and Frosty Mitchell who was a friend of mine at Drake—I got him a job there after I was working there, and he went on to be one of the well-known owners and broadcasters in the state of Iowa for many, many years. So, I did get to do play-by-play, and it was at KWDM.

I kept a scrapbook of things I cut out of the newspaper and magazines concerning sports and athletes. One of my early favorite players was Bob Kurland. Bob was a seven-footer at Oklahoma A&M (now Oklahoma State). It was so much fun to finally meet Bob Kurland when I went back to the Basketball Hall of Fame to get my award. We had a great conversation. He appreciated it. He's retired and in his 80s now. George Mikan, who was at DePaul, and Don Otten, at Bowling Green, were a couple more of basketball's first really tall centers who could play.

I followed the **UNIVERSITY OF IOWA*** teams a lot then. They had Dave Danner, Dick Ives and the Wilkinson brothers. Murray Wier was a favorite, but he came a little later. The very first player I ever saw dunk the basketball was Gaylord Anderson at Iowa State. He was 6'4" and was the only player on the team who could dunk the ball. Everybody came early to watch him dunk in warm-ups. This was probably about 1948. In those days, no one could dunk the basketball, and he didn't play much for Iowa State. But he was a favorite in pregame activities, because he

*In 1939, the Heisman Trophy winner was Nile Kinnick of **IOWA**. He is the only Heisman Trophy winner to have his university's football stadium named after him. In 1934, Nile Kinnick was Bob Feller's catcher on an American Legion baseball team.

could dunk. Basketball was played on a different level then. It was played more on the floor, with passing, cutting, running, and shooting. In today's game, with all the great leapers, they play above the rim. It was a different game at that time. We didn't have the big scoring, and it was a more deliberately played game.

ANDY PAFKO* was my favorite baseball player. I would listen to the Chicago Cubs. The first game I ever saw at Wrigley Field was the Cubs versus the **PHILADELPHIA PHILLIES*** in 1945. I was fortunate enough to see a World Series game that year with Detroit. When I went to that first game, it was with one of my cousins. He ran down to get autographs of the players. I just wanted to see where Bert Wilson, the famous Cubs announcer, was broadcasting the game.

A number of years later, here in Phoenix, when there weren't as many spring training games, they used to have an annual spring training luncheon in Scottsdale. They asked me to be the emcee. The speaker that year was former Cub manager Charlie Grimm. When I introduced Charlie, I said, "Charlie, just so you'll remember: Phil Cavarretta at first base, Don Johnson at second, Stan Hack at third, Lennie Merullo at shortstop, Harry 'Peanuts' Lowrey in left, 'Handy Andy' Pafko in center, Bill Nicholson in right, Clyde McCullough behind the plate and Hank Borowy on the mound." Charlie started to cry. That was his 1945 Cubs team. To me, no one was better than "Handy Andy" Pafko, the kid from Boyceville, Wisconsin.

My family had a distant cousin that lived in Serena, Illinois. They were Cubs season ticket holders and big fans. That's how I got to my first game and how we got to the World Series. All my

*In the very first set of Topps baseball cards, the first card (#1) was **ANDY PAFKO**.

*P. K. Wrigley and Milton Hershey were bitter business rivals. When Wrigley bought the Chicago Cubs, Hershey tried to buy the **PHILADELPHIA PHILLIES**...and sell chocolate gum. Hershey failed in both efforts.

classmates were excited about my getting to go to a World Series game. They wanted to hear all about it. To get the chance to go to those games as a kid was just unbelievable. My best friend in high school was Dick Knickerbocker. We were the starting guards on the basketball team. He's now a retired teacher and coach living in California. We still talk all the time. We listened to Cubs games together every single day. We'd hear the Cubs game, and then we'd go out and play baseball.

When I walked into **WRIGLEY FIELD***, I felt like I'd been there a hundred times, because I'd heard Bert Wilson describe everything in that ball park, especially the ivy-covered wall. I remember hearing "Bill Nicholson hits one out over right field. It's outta here! A carton of Old Gold cigarettes goes to the veterans' hospital down in Pekin, Illinois!" There were vendors selling programs and pencils. I was walking ahead of my dad saying, "I'll take a program. I'll take a...." My dad saw me and yelled, "Hey, hold it up there. I'm running out of money." I thought everything was going to be free at the old ball park.

Most of my friends were Cubs fans, too, because we got their broadcasts in Williams. We got the Cardinals' broadcasts also, and, of course, that was Harry Caray. For some reason, the Cubs were the team we seemed to gravitate to. Naturally, I had to tell all the stories about how it was at Wrigley Field. My friends would ask, "How are the seats? Did it really have all that 'ivy stuff' on the wall?"

During my senior year in high school, our basketball team ran off a win streak of 15 or 16 games in a row. One of the schools we played was Woolstock. They had one of the biggest players around. He was 6' 7" or 6'8." In those days nobody had players that big, even in college. He was having a field day with us. We

*More NFL GAMES have been played in the Meadowlands than any other stadium. Until 2003, **WRIGLEY FIELD** held the record even though Wrigley had not hosted an NFL game since 1971.

had nobody to match up with him and just couldn't stop this guy. During a timeout in the second half, Coach Lovin said, "Anybody want to try this guy?" I said, "I'll try him." I'm 5'7". We had only one referee in high school basketball in those days. I got behind this big guy. When he'd post up, when it looked like they were going to throw the ball to him, I'd just grab his trunks and hang on. The official was out in front so he couldn't see whether I had my hands on him or not. When the guy would get the ball, I'd be holding him so he'd be off balance, and if he threw a shot up, it didn't go. This worked for three or four possessions. Finally, the referee figured something had to be going on in there. The referee called a timeout, and he walked over to me, and said, "I don't know what you're doing, but if I see what you're doing, you're not going to be playing any more in this game." That ended that. Years later, I'm in Denver to do a Phoenix Suns game. Just before the game, I see this big, tall guy coming up to me. He said, "You're Al McCoy? I don't know if you remember me, but I went to Woolstock High School and played basketball against you." He's now a ranger in the forest service in Colorado. He said, "You're the guy who played me the toughest defensively, because you held onto my shorts!"

When we were on our winning streak, we played a school called Owasa. These small towns have tiny gyms, and everybody in the town went to the games. The fans could get pretty rabid. Owasa had a winning streak going, too. The game turned into a knock-down, drag-out battle. The referee couldn't control it. Everyone was going to the floor. Guys were getting knocked against the wall. Fans were coming out on the floor. Finally, in the closing seconds, we win the game. As we're running off the floor, Coach Lovin says, "No showers. Grab your clothes. Get on the bus. We're getting out of here." The next day, our superintendent called Owasa and said, "We're not coming there to play anymore." But we won the game.

When I was 14, I'd spend many nights going around and playing with a band in ballrooms. It was a new experience for me. This was a time when a lot of musicians were being drafted into the military, so bands were looking for piano players. There was a knock on the door one day at my farmhouse. Jimmy Dunlap was at the door and wanted to know if Al McCoy was there. My mother called me over, and he said, "I've got the band at the VFW Club in a nearby town. We play Wednesday through Saturday nights, and I need a piano player. If you're interested, come on over Wednesday night, and if you can cut it, you'll get the job." I thought, "What the heck?" If I could keep everything going in school, I'd be excited about the opportunity. I had to join the union, and I believe scale was $7 a night. I went over and sat in and got the job. It was Jimmy Dunlap and the Collegians. I wasn't a collegian, yet, and most of the other guys were either guys who had been in the service and were out, or of that age, so it was an indoctrination for me. We were a five-piece group, as I remember. We started playing all over that area. The entire time I was in high school, I continued to play with that band.

I never went to a junior or senior prom because I was always playing dance jobs. That $28 a week was big money back then and helped me pay for college later on. This is when I really became interested in the big bands. When I started playing with them, I was nervous about whether or not I could do the job adequately. The first night, Jimmy Dunlap gave me arrangements and music, and I sat in and played.

I got an interesting letter from one of the territory bands when I was a senior, offering me $48 a week to go on the road. I didn't take that job, because I was going to Drake University. When I started at Drake, during the first week or two, I met a guy in my class. We started talking about music, and he said, "I play with the Eddie Allen band," which was a well-known territory band out of Ames, Iowa. He said they were looking for a piano player. They broadcast on radio every Saturday afternoon, so I went up, met Eddie Allen, and sat in with the band. I started playing with him and, a short time later, with another territory group called the Don Hoy band.

Territory band was a commonly used term in the Midwest among musicians in those days. These were bands that normally had three brass, three reeds, three rhythm, and a singer, and they worked a whole territory—Iowa, Illinois, Missouri, the Dakotas, and Nebraska. Lawrence Welk had a territory band at that time.

All the time I was at Drake University, I mostly worked with either Eddie Allen or Don Hoy. We'd sometimes travel three to four hours to play. Sometimes in the summer, we might be gone for 10 days to two weeks, working ballrooms throughout the Midwest.

In those days, in Iowa, the clubs had everything—gambling, liquor, you name it. One time the cocktail waitress came over and asked me what I wanted to drink. All the older guys ordered what they wanted. I wasn't too familiar with what to drink, but I'd heard somebody say "Tom Collins." So I said, "Give me a Tom Collins." Pretty soon the cocktail waitress comes over and gives me the Tom Collins. She's a pretty attractive gal. I set this big glass of Tom Collins down on the end of the piano and looked up at the girl and said, "I don't want to see that empty tonight." Well, I have to tell you, by intermission I was having a tough time finding the keyboard. That was my first experience, and maybe my last, with Tom Collins. You have to realize that a lot of young guys were in bands in those days. Stan Getz, for example, who went on to become one of the great jazz players in the country, joined Woody Herman when he was 16. It wasn't unusual for bands to have very, very young players.

It was an adventure traveling on the road with territory bands. We played the Corn Palace in Mitchell, South Dakota, one winter. We had to help unload the equipment from the bus. I didn't realize how cold it was. I found out later it was 15 degrees below zero. I didn't have gloves on or anything. When I went in to start playing, part of my fingers were still frozen, and I had a tough time trying to play that night. I got frostbitten and didn't realize it.

I really like music. I like the big bands and jazz. I enjoyed playing, which I still do. But I realized very early that being a musician was a tough life. I met a lot of great, great musicians who were fabulous players, but they either had alcohol or drug problems or maybe they just couldn't make it. In those days marijuana was prevalent. And Dexedrine was present. But they were starting in then on the heavier drugs, too, like heroin. I had the realization early that although I enjoyed playing in bands, this probably wasn't going to be the end-all of my career.

We used to kid musicians, because there were always certain gals who liked the trumpet players. And certain gals who liked the saxophone players. And, thankfully, there were a few who liked the piano players.

I don't think my classmates had much interest in my playing with the band. They knew that I was out doing this, but they didn't think that much about it. My mom, however, thought I was going to be on *The Lawrence Welk Show*. Lawrence Welk had his territory band and was getting pretty well known.

Playing with the dance bands and working in radio really helped me get through college financially. It might seem funny to today's college students, but during my junior year at Drake, I was carrying a full load for the semester, pulling a radio shift, and playing with the band. All my classes were in the morning, starting at seven o'clock. At noon, I'd go to the cafeteria, and a lady would have a sandwich made up for me. I'd go down to WHO radio, where I worked from one to six in the afternoon. At six o'clock, I raced home to change clothes, because they picked me up to play a dance at least four nights a week. I'd get home maybe at two o'clock in the morning and then get up for that seven o'clock class. I got my best grades that semester. Figure that out!

The musicians were such a great group of guys. There used to be a place in Creston, Iowa, called the Chicken Shack. Every band, from big bands to territory bands to combos, played the Chicken Shack. It was a long way from anywhere, down in the southern part of the state. A lot of guys didn't want to make that trip because it was two-and-a-half hours each way. After I had almost quit playing with the Eddie Allen band and was with Don Hoy, mostly in Des Moines, Eddie would still call me to play with his band if I wasn't working. He'd call and say, "Listen, I'm going to the Chicken Shack in Creston on Thursday night. I need a piano man." I'd say, "Eddie, I'm not going down there. I've got an early class." "Aw, we'll come back right after the gig. I'll pay you double scale." Those guys in that band were the worst. When the job was over, they'd argue and drink, and we'd never leave. But finally I'd say, "Okay, I'll go." Now, we play 'til one o'clock, and I want to be home by 3:30. when the job was over, we'd be down in the band room changing clothes, and Eddie's arguing with the guys about why they played such and such a tune and such and such a set. These guys were unbelievable. Anyhow, he was the only guy who could play trumpet and smoke at the same time. I don't know how he did it, but he did. My all-time favorite big bands: 1) Count Basie, 2) Woody Herman's 4 Brothers Band. Also Kenton and Ellington.

I never heard Ronald Reagan when he was on the radio on WHO in Des Moines. He was just a little bit ahead of me when I got involved in listening. The guys I mostly listened to were the national guys like Bill Stern, who did college football every Saturday and did *The Colgate Sports Newsreel* on Friday nights. And Don Dunphy, who did those great fights—all the Joe Louis and Billy Conn fights. In later years, I had an opportunity to meet both Bill Stern and Don Dunphy, and, to me, even though it was in the very late stages of their careers, it was a tremendous thrill just to meet them.

I graduated from Drake University in 1954. I was working at KWDM radio in Des Moines. I left WHO, because I knew I'd never get Jim Zabel's job. Jim did Iowa sports from the beginning of time and has always been a great broadcaster and friend. One night, shortly after we had graduated from Drake, a friend and I were sitting around, and we said, "Let's go to California."

My friend said, "I've got a sister who lives in Albuquerque. When we get that far, we'll stay there." I said, "I've got cousins who just moved to Phoenix. We'll stay there." I went in the next day, resigned my position at KWDM, and we hung around for another week. Then we jumped in my car and headed west. When you're that young, you're not afraid of anything.

We were going to check things out and look for jobs. We got to Liberal, Kansas, and stayed there during a tornado warning. We got to Albuquerque, and my friend's sister and husband were there. We had just gotten to Albuquerque when my friend's dad called from Chicago to tell him he had gotten his draft notice. So he had to go back to Chicago. Since I had cousins in Phoenix, I wanted to continue there.

I'd heard about Phoenix, but didn't know what to expect. I knew it was out in the desert. I had been in communication with my cousins, who had been there eight months, and they liked living there. I moved in with them and started hitting the radio stations looking for a job. They wouldn't even talk to me. I couldn't even get an interview with anybody. It was really disheartening. Finally, I was going to leave. I happened to be in a bar called Pings, which was on 16th Street and Camelback, that had a piano. I asked the bartender if it would be okay for me to play the piano. He said, "Yeah, our guy just left, and they're looking for somebody." I wound up playing piano at Pings for about six weeks. Eventually, I left and went to **DENVER*** to look for a TV or radio job there. It was the same situation—I couldn't get anything.

I went back to Des Moines. By this time, it was late August, and I didn't have anything to do, so I put a trio together and went into a key club called the Green Parrot. That was before they had liquor by the drink in Iowa. They had these key clubs, but

*In the upper deck at Coors Field in **DENVER**, there is a row of seats that is painted purple all the way around the stadium to signify the mile-high altitude level.

to get in, you had to pay a fee to have your own key and, supposedly, your own bottle. These were all over Des Moines at that time. We worked four nights a week. A couple of weeks later, I'm walking down the street in Des Moines, and I meet John Ross Winnie, who recognized me, but I did not recognize him. I'd had his sister as a grammar school teacher in Williams. He was on the faculty at the University of Iowa in their Broadcast Communications Department. We talked, and he said, "What are you doing?" I was embarrassed to tell him I was working as a musician. He asked me if I ever thought about going to graduate school. I hadn't. He said, "I'll tell you what. We've got a graduate assistantship available. I know you can get it. Just come down for an interview. You'll get books, tuition, and be paid a stipend for stuff you do for the university. Why don't you do it?" Now, this was one week before classes. At that time, TV was in its infancy, and the only TV station in Iowa was WOI-TV in Ames.

I drove down to Iowa City and do the interview. After it's done, Professor Winnie comes over and says, "Well, you're in. You're all set." I said, "Where am I going to live?" He said, "Go over to Housing. They'll give you a list of places, and you can find yourself an apartment or whatever you want."

Well, in Iowa City a week before classes started, you can imagine what was on that list. I looked at places I wouldn't even consider living in. At the end of the day, I said, "This is ridiculous. If I can't find a decent place to live, I'm not coming down here." I had two places left on my list, so the decision I had to make was, "Do I go back to Des Moines and write it off?" or "Do I stay overnight in Iowa City and check out these final two places?"

It was eight o'clock at night, and I didn't want to drive back to Des Moines so I went to a motel in Iowa City. The next day I got up, had breakfast, and saw 310 Golf View Avenue on the list. It sounded interesting, so I drove over. Here's this street of beautiful ranch-style homes that overlooked the old golf course in Iowa City. I pulled up to the house and knocked on the door. It belonged to a couple who owned a drug store in Iowa City.

Their son was in medical school. The couple was leaving for their home in Florida and wouldn't come back until May 1. Their son wanted to get a couple of guys to live with him in the house. He already had one guy who was in law school and thought he had another guy, but he backed out. Well, there I was!

The home was unbelievable. The whole downstairs was finished off in knotty pine. It had everything you can imagine. I said, "This is for me!" On the same street was Bucky O'Connor, the head basketball coach, and Forest Evashevski, the head football coach. I had a great year in graduate school there.

The second day of classes I met Jim Colston, who had just gotten out of the service and was back to finish up his undergraduate degree. We were talking, and the subject got to radio, and he said, "I've got a job at KXIC, the local radio station, and they're looking for another announcer." I go down, meet the program director, and get hired on the spot.

So now I'm working at KXIC, the commercial radio station in Iowa City. I've got a graduate assistantship at the university. I wound up helping monitor a freshman class in history and appreciation of the movies. That was one of my big contributions there. Then, about three weeks later, I ran into a guy that's playing in a band, so I also wound up playing dance jobs. If I hadn't been walking down the street a few months earlier, my life would have been dramatically different.

When I was at Iowa in 1955, basketball was big. The basketball team went to the Final Four in Kansas City that year with "Cool" Carl Cain, Deacon Davis, Sharm Scheuerman, Bill Logan and Bill Seaberg. It was Colorado, LaSalle, San Francisco, and Iowa. I went and sent reports back to the station from Kansas City. Bill Russell was the first basketball player I had ever seen who could get the ball under the basket and do a reverse dunk.

When I see Bill Russell today, and we've known each other since his playing and coaching days, I always go up and whisper in his ear, "I could tell everybody you wore a little green hat for the San

Francisco Dons in Kansas City." He gives me that cackle laugh of his. Bill Russell dominated that tournament. No one had ever seen a player like him. He could block shots and rebound. He could do it all. K.C. Jones was also on their team. Phil Woolpert was the coach. They were terrific. Iowa was good that year, but San Francisco was dominant.

In 1954, I was finishing up at Drake and working at KWDM. Dick Nesbitt, who had been a kicker for the **CHICAGO BEARS*** after starring at Drake, was now a sports director at WOR in New York, and had come back to Des Moines, because his father had passed away. Dick had to take a leave of absence for several weeks from his job to come back to settle up the estate. He heard me doing the play-by-play of a game and came out to the station one afternoon and introduced himself. We became friends while he was there and would get together occasionally.

I'm in Iowa City, and I get a call from Dick just before the football season starts. He says, "Listen, I just changed jobs, and I'm at WJJD in Chicago. We're going to be doing a college football game of the week, 'I Pick It,' sponsored by Sinclair Oil. I'd like to have you help me out." That gave me a boost. I did some production and a little on-the-air work. On some weekends, I'd fly to whatever game we were doing.

Some of the games we did were Iowa, Notre Dame, SMU, **TEXAS***, Michigan and Michigan State. At the same time, he introduced me to the management and program people at WJJD, and I was able to do a little fill-in work there also.

*The **CHICAGO BEARS** wear blue and orange because those are the colors that team founder George Halas wore when he played for the University of Illinois.

*When **TEXAS** hired Mack Brown, he became the highest paid coach in college football history even though he had never won a conference championship.

Dick Nesbitt ended up leaving his job in Chicago and going to Channel 5 in Minneapolis, KSTP-TV. He'd never done TV in his life. Again, he wanted me to go with him and be in the sports department there, but I didn't do it. Dick was a great big heavy-set guy who wore thick, solid glasses. He became an institution in Minneapolis. He'd go on the air smoking his pipe, talking sports. Everybody loved him.

I was starting to think about what I might want to do. One of the reasons I had gone to graduate school in Iowa was because of their TV/cinematography department and all its equipment, cameras, studios, etc. I got a real indoctrination into television, so that year at Iowa was definitely worthwhile for me.

When I was at WHO, I wanted to do a piano/disc jockey show like *The Steve Allen Show*. I did an audition at WHO for their program people. Everybody loved it, but they wound up letting a professional piano player on their staff, Bill Austin, do the show. He wasn't an announcer, and it wasn't a very good show.

With Dick Nesbitt leaving, I was losing my contact there, but still working at KXIC. I put a couple of ads in *Broadcasting Magazine*, which used to have a section where announcers could place ads. I placed one looking for a sports job, play-by-play, etc. Then, I got to thinking, when I was at WHO in Des Moines, I did a tape with a disc jockey show playing piano. It was similar to a Steve Allen type show where I played piano between records and segued into the records. I was trying to get that going at WHO at that time, and they decided not to do it and gave it to another one of their older musicians who was there to do that type of show. He didn't do it very well, but he did it. So, I decided to put an ad in for that also. That's the one I got a reply on from a station in Buffalo, New York, WHLD, who had studios in Buffalo in the Peter Stuyvescant Hotel and in the Hotel Niagara in Niagara Falls. They hired me to do a piano, disc jockey show.

GYM DANDY

Chuck Lovin

Chuck Lovin coached and taught at Williams High School in Iowa from 1946 through 1951. He then moved to a much larger high school in nearby Boone, the hometown of First Lady Mamie Eisenhower. Coach Lovin's wife, Lorraine, also taught at Williams. Coach Lovin and Al McCoy have remained close friends over the years. He's an avid golfer and spends part of every year in the Phoenix area.

I've lived in Boone, Iowa, for almost 60 years. I coached at a school here for 34 years. But my relationship with Al McCoy goes back even further than that. I first saw young Al McCoy 63 years ago when he came into Williams High School as a ninth grader.

My wife and I went together for eight years—four years in college at Iowa and the four years I was in the war before I came home—and then we got married. Both of us got jobs in Williams, Iowa. I've got to give my wife as much credit as me for helping Al, because she taught English and speech and had him participate in all the school plays. She's as good an English teacher as they've ever had in the state of Iowa. The kids knew their English, because she drilled them when they were in ninth grade, and then she moved with them when they went on to the tenth grade.

When I first got to Williams, we had a bunch of seniors. They hadn't had a real coach in four years, because of the war. Some farmer coached them during that time. All the kids were smoking. I took them on, but I was already looking at the ninth grade. That was the future. There were seven boys in that class, and Al was one of them. I said, "That's my next team after I get rid of these seniors."

I pounded those seniors and, believe it or not, we won the Sectional tournament and went to District, playing in those little gyms. When our seniors got in the District tournament, when Al was a freshman, we went to the Armory at Iowa State and the kids were just amazed, because it was so big. Al said he never would forget it.

My brother was a junior in high school at Hansel, and the superintendent let me take my team over there to play a practice game. Al always remembers that. He said, "I remember you took us back to where you starred." I had played four years on the team, and we had lost one game... when I was in ninth grade. I played with four seniors, and the team that beat us was the tallest team in the state of Iowa, New Hartford.

When our Williams team made it to the Armory for District play, we played like a house afire for about a third of the game, but that was the end. Their rear ends were dragging. All that smoking had taken its toll. Now, I was looking forward to this young bunch coming up. They weren't going to be smoking.

They were all good kids. Al was a typical Iowa kid, I would say. Everything he did was intense. If he was in a school play, he played it right to the hilt. He was an outstanding basketball player. When I played him at guard, not many people got around him. When he shot a free throw, he made it. He was a good shooter.

By the time Al was a senior, I'd had that group together for three years. They took their lumps when they were sophomores because they were the starting team. Six out of the seven kids in that class played basketball, and that was my entire team. When they got to be seniors, they were pretty good playing together. I'd take them outside and practice screening and other things. Then we'd get in those little gyms, and we were on top of each other.

I just looked at our record. I knew we had won a lot. Al said, "Look here Coach, we won 15 straight games." I said, "Yeah, but we lost the next four in a row." Anyway, Al's bunch won a lot of games.

Al was good at psyching up his teammates. When he was a ninth grader, he sat on the bench with the rest of his group. He would sit there and announce the game underneath his breath. If we got ahead a little bit, since I knew that was my team for the next three years, I'd put them in. Al was very intense about everything. He was a terrific guy.

> ...he sat on the bench with the rest of his group. He would sit there and announce the game underneath his breath.

Al was 5'7" in high school. His running mate was Dick Knickerbocker, and they are still very good friends. We've kept in contact with those guys for 60 years now. They just are terrific people. I'll put those guys up against anyone in the state of Iowa. They were tremendous kids.

Al graduated in 1950, and when Williams High had their 50th reunion, the whole class was there. They also invited the Lovins to spend the weekend with them. That was something special. The feelings I have about those kids...see, I had gone from Williams, a little Class B school, to Boone, the biggest AA school in the state, and it was Al's bunch that helped me get there.

Al McCoy is one of the best basketball announcers in the United States. He's so much better than Billy Packer and the rest of those guys. Al was a very fine piano player and even played on television in Phoenix. We've been retired 27 years, and we'd often go to Phoenix until I had a heart attack about 10 years ago. Al would give us tickets to watch the Suns. Then, after the game, he'd take me in to meet the Suns coaches. We'd visit and go out to have a beer at some of his favorite places. He's just a common, ordinary guy, but they just lay out the red carpet for him—free drinks and the dessert tray!

Now that Al is getting older, I just feel like he's a brother. Back in the school days, we didn't have to discipline the kids. If there was a problem, the kids would usually take care of it and straighten things out themselves. In a small town, you have a little better handle on things. You're closely knitted together. That's what I told these kids just the other day, "You know, for years, I've been in this big double A school here, but I told people a thousand times that I would put you Williams kids up against any kids we had." We had a lot of smart kids. That's the difference. When you have a PTA in these little schools, the parents would get all dressed up and come to the meetings. If you wanted to talk to one of them, they were there for their kids. In the bigger schools, we didn't even have PTA. You didn't have the same closeness. Bigness is not the answer to education. I told the kids that we had three couples at Williams: the superintendent and his wife, another couple, and Lorraine and I, and we all taught our classes. We all worked together.

On Sunday mornings, everybody went to a church. It didn't make any difference which church, but most were Catholic. Most of the people in town also went to the ball games. If there was a school play or a game, everyone would turn out. They'd put on their Sunday best. You don't see that today.

Al graduated in 1950, and I left Williams in 1951.

Lorraine and I are just amazed when we come to Phoenix and see Al interviewing the basketball stars and realize how far he has come. He handles it so well. He doesn't feel like he's a big shot. He's so unassuming. Even on television, he brags about being from the little town of Williams all the time.

Al had a golf outing that he put on. He invited me to play in it as his guest. He told me to be at his place at nine o'clock in the morning. I pulled in and here's this big limo. I'd never been in a limo. We had sandwiches, beer, whatever we wanted. They had a big crowd with all the Suns playing and had a band playing. I played with two of Al's sons and the trainer, Joe Proski. We just had a great time. That night, the band asked Al to get up and play the piano. Al told me to sit down, and he'd be back in awhile. I'm sitting there and here comes this long-haired guy, and I didn't know who he was. Turns out he was Alice Cooper. I'd heard them over the intercom all day talking about Alice, and I thought, "There aren't any women playing—they're all men. Who's this Alice?" I didn't know who he was. But I've never forgotten him. Now, when I see him on television, I can say, "There's **ALICE COOPER!***"

To me, there never was any doubt that Al McCoy would be successful. We knew he'd be in radio. He started out in Webster City at KJFJ when he was at Drake. Every year, he comes back and spends a day or two with us. The last two or three times, I've set up a coffee get-together in Williams for him. I call some of the people who were in his class, and we all get together to visit.

When I drive back into Williams, there's a feeling I can't explain, but I have a feeling of pride. One time, when I was giving a speech to them, I told them, "You're the guys who gave me the confidence so I could go to a bigger school and realize that I can coach. You're the reason I've been successful." I still have a great feeling for them, and my wife feels the same way.

---

*The band, Pearl Jam, was originally named Mookie Blaylock, after the former Oklahoma and NBA player. They recorded their first album, "Ten" under that name. In 1992, the band Mookie Blaylock changed their name to Pearl Jam after a hallucinogenic concoction made by lead **SINGER** Eddie Vedder's great-grandmother, Pearl.

Chapter 2

SHUFFLIN' OFF TO BUFFALO

Save $$ on Your Honeymoon— Marry a Niagara Falls Gal

After I ran my ads in the broadcasting magazines, I got a quick reply from WHLD in Buffalo, New York. A few days later, I'm in Buffalo. The station had studios at Hotel Stuyvesant in Buffalo and Hotel Niagara in Niagara Falls.

On July 4, 1956, I was on the air in a huge studio in the Hotel Niagara, with a beautiful grand piano, doing a piano/DJ show. The show worked. Everybody had a one-year deal, but before the year was up, a guy who had managed the station before convinced the owner that these guys were spending all his money, and it wasn't going to work. Ownership decided to change everything. All of us who were there that year eventually left. When I heard about the format changes coming, I got very nervous. "Now where's the next step going to be," I wondered.

At my first broadcasting job in Webster City, Iowa, the general manager told me that the guys who get ahead in this business are the ones who know where their next job is. I have to tell you, I was a little shook up that this change was coming. I thought we had been doing a good job, which we had, but we had been spending an awful lot of money on promotion and that proved to be our downfall. My friend, Jim Colston, whom I had worked with in Iowa City, was now working at a radio station in Estherville, Iowa. The owner was about to start a new station in Minneapolis. He got in touch with me, asking me to come back. "We'll go to the new station in Minneapolis," he said. So, I still had a contact.

Buffalo is a great place. I met a lot of people there who are still my friends. When you are doing broadcast work, people love you. Besides doing this piano/disc jockey show, I also did sports. I did a sportscast every evening on the station. The first week I was on the air—remember when Western Union had guys on bicycles delivering telegrams?—I had just finished my show and a Western Union guy pulls up with a bottle of high-priced Scotch delivered from one of the biggest bookies in the area. He wanted to have the right to call me and ask, "Who's hurt? Who's injured? Who's not playing?"

I developed some great friendships in Buffalo and Niagara Falls. I lived in a small apartment between the two cities, since we had studios in both places. There are a lot of terrific Italian people in that area and some great Italian restaurants—I could have pasta three times a day! I met everybody—from the chief of police on down. It was a great year.

Even though I was still a young guy, I had a lot of experience. Naturally, I was nervous about going off to work at a place I'd never been. I wondered how everything would work out since I took the job without even seeing the situation there. Everything had been done on the phone. Two guys had taken over the station to really promote it and had hired all the top people in Buffalo. Some of the disc jockeys were Tom Clay; Lucky Pierre, who went on to Los Angeles to have a big career; and Rick Azar, who eventually became the dominant TV sportscaster in Buffalo. They hired all the top people, and we promoted them like crazy.

> I met my wife-to-be in the third week I was in Buffalo.

I met my wife-to-be in the third week I was in Buffalo. On First Street, the same street the Hotel Niagara was on in downtown Niagara Falls, was a beauty shop and a nice little bar, Frenchy's Grill, that had great food. Frenchy's became my hangout, because I had met the owner, Vince Corriere, and we became very good friends. We were both single guys. He was going with a gal whose dad owned this beauty shop. He was having a birthday party, and I accepted his invitation to attend. My wife, who at that time was working as a cosmetologist, was at the birthday party. And, oh yes, there was a piano there, so during the evening, I started playing. I look around and standing behind me is this very beautiful, dark-haired, brown-eyed, Armenian young lady named Georgia Shahinian. I thought she was attractive, and we spent some time together getting acquainted. I found out where she worked, so almost every day some of us would walk down to have lunch, and I'd look in this place and give her a wave. A week or so later, I asked her out to dinner. She took me home, and her mother had shish kabobs and rice pilaf and all those Armenian goodies. What are you going to do?

My relationship with Georgia moved along pretty quickly. I had so much respect for her and her family. She had just lost her father a few months earlier. Her mom was still there. She had a twin sister and another sister. I just found her so comfortable to be around. Before you know it, we were spending an awful lot of time together. When the word came out that my radio deal was going to be bought out, and I would be doing something else, we had to talk about the future.

During my year in Buffalo, I'd gone down to New York to see baseball's **NEW YORK GIANTS*** play. That's when I met Eddie Brannick and Russ Hodges, the announcer. Russ is the one who tipped me off that the Giants were moving to San Francisco, and the Dodgers were definitely going to L.A. The rumors of the moves were very strong at that time, but what wasn't known was that Giants' owner Horace Stoneham was going to move his Minneapolis farm club to Phoenix. This was a big deal then, because at one time, Minneapolis thought they were going to get the big club. That wasn't known then.

I don't know why they decided to move the team, but I do know the spring training site had previously been moved to Phoenix. It's just my opinion that Horace Stoneham liked having his AAA team where spring training was held.

Georgia and I decided we were going to get married. I told her that we would be moving, but I didn't know where. Georgia was very family oriented and had never been west of Detroit. This would be a huge move for her.

*In 1916, the **GIANTS** had a 26-game winning streak. When they started the streak, they were in fourth place and when they finally lost, they were still in fourth place.

Remember, I had a cousin in Phoenix. An uncle of mine had also moved to Phoenix in the interim. Now, with a cousin and an uncle in Phoenix, I'm talking about moving there because the AAA team is going to be there, too. I thought I had a shot at getting a job with the club, and Russ Hodges also thought so.

When I'd go down to New York from Buffalo in the summer to Giants baseball games, I'd get press credentials and get in the press box area, where I happened to meet Russ. Interestingly enough, Eddie Brannick, who they used to refer to as the "Little Shepherd of the Press," took a liking to me. You never know how people are going to react to you. I went to Giants games at the Polo Grounds and was at **EBBETS FIELD*** one time. Both were old and historic. They didn't have the amenities ball parks have today. It was a thrill to go to games there.

Now a lot of things had to happen in a hurry. Georgia and I decided we were going to be married. We knew we were going to be moving someplace. In the meantime, my friends in Iowa were anxious for me to come there. Finally, we made the decision to go to Iowa for six to eight weeks because Georgia had never met a lot of my friends or relatives. Then, we would go on to Phoenix. They had me work at the station in Estherville, Iowa, 15 miles away from Emmetsburg, where one of my best college friends owned a hotel and a restaurant. He got me an apartment there. They put a piano in one of the rooms, and I did a morning broadcast from there.

I went to Iowa to get things set up. In the meantime, all of Georgia's friends were saying, "He's never coming back." They thought it was all a big scam. I was in Iowa for only a week or so before we set a wedding date. I worked there until we were married on

*Only 6,700 fans attended the Dodgers' finale at **EBBETS FIELD** in 1957. The park—built 44 years earlier—had a capacity of 32,000 with only 700 parking spaces. An apartment building now sits on that site.

June 23, 1956. We had the wedding, we had the reception, and we were out the door for a little Canadian honeymoon.

In those days, Niagara Falls was amazing. The downtown was booming for a lot of reasons. They didn't have liquor by the drink in Canada then. So many people came to Niagara Falls and Buffalo for entertainment. Sadly, that has changed, and downtown Niagara is way down. It's a shame. The Town Casino in Buffalo was a beautiful nightclub, a Vegas-type club owned by Harry Altman. They had Nat King Cole and Sammy Davis, Jr., and all the big names there. I loved it and even did some broadcasts from there.

We headed off to Iowa, and my wife had never been there. She fell in love with it. She met all my friends and family. We knew we were going to go to Phoenix—it was just a matter of setting a time to do it. We stayed in Iowa about two months, cruising around in my '54 Ford with no air conditioning.

Chapter 3

BY THE TIME
I GOT TO PHOENIX

The Valley of the Sun...
Except in the Summer When
It's the Surface of the Sun

eorgia and I were finally heading for Phoenix. I had talked to my uncle, and he said we could stay with them until we got settled. We decided to take a chance. I was going to have to apply for the Phoenix Giants job. I had learned there were two stations the Giants were talking to, KOY and KOOL. If the Phoenix job didn't work out, I still had an opportunity with that new station in Minneapolis.

It was early in September 1956, and I was driving the '54 Ford, pulling a trailer holding all our stuff. We stayed in Albuquerque and then continued on to Phoenix. They were just putting in the road in the canyon. They were blasting, and we got held up. I swore I'd never drive there again. Remember, we had no air conditioning. As we're coming into Phoenix, my wife, who usually doesn't complain, kept saying, "Is it always this hot here?" I'm giving her the old story, "It's a dry heat."

Finally, we get to Mesa, and she says, "We've got to stop. I have got to have something to drink, lemonade or iced tea." She got out of the car, and then I realized that the heater had been on, but only on her side! The vents were closed on my side. She had not only been getting the outside air but the air from the heater, too! I didn't tell her that for about 20 years.

I knew that one of those two stations would get the Phoenix Giants broadcasts, so I went to both. I went to KOY and gave them all my tapes. Bill Close was the guy in charge there. Bill was very tough to interview with. He listened to some of my play-by-play tapes, and when I went back to ask him about them, he said, "Yeah, is that it?" I said, "That's it. That's my act." Then I went to KOOL, where Homer Lane was the program director. Horace Stoneham was a good friend of Tom Chauncey, who, along with Gene Autry, owned what was then KOOL radio and television. Homer Lane offered me the job, and right after I had taken it, I got a call from Bill Close with a job offer at KOY. I told him I'd already taken the job at KOOL, because they were going to do the Phoenix Giants.

Before the baseball was a reality, I did several other things at KOOL. I had a live nighttime radio show from 10 p.m. until 2 a.m. Then they replayed it from 2 to 6 a.m. It was sponsored by Courtesy Chevrolet. Since it ran back to back, we couldn't give the time. We'd have to say "10 past the hour" or "20 minutes before the hour." I joked that the good thing about it was that on the way home, I got to listen to myself.

By then, my wife was pregnant with our first son. I did that night show for about two months, and then I was switched to early mornings. And I started doing baseball. When the Phoenix Giants came, they played at an old ball park at South Central and Mojave.

Rosy Ryan, who had been the team's general manager in Minneapolis, was the GM in Phoenix. At one time Ryan had been **BABE RUTH***'s roommate. He was a solid baseball guy and taught me so much about broadcasting baseball.

The city, as it has been known to do, made a commitment that they would build a new ball park. Two years later, they still hadn't even put a shovel in the ground. Horace Stoneham got a little upset. Tacoma, Washington, had built a new ball park, and the team was going to move there. In the old ball park, Rosy Ryan used to tell the story that every time a foul ball hit the roof all the toilets flushed in the whole building. The press box was just up above with chicken wire in front, and the writers and broadcasters were all there in the same place.

I had the distinction of being involved in the only game in baseball history that was postponed because of grasshoppers. My first summer there, the city of Phoenix was inundated by grasshoppers. It was almost like driving around in snow. There'd be a drift of grasshoppers on the street. You'd start sliding around on the road. One night at the ball park, all these grasshoppers

*In Babe Ruth's first major league game—as a pitcher for the Boston Red Sox—he was removed in the 7th inning for a pinch hitter.

surrounded the lights and cut off all the light. They had to postpone the game.

Art Gleason, during those first three years, was really the number-one announcer. Art had worked the "Mutual Game of the Day" and other major league stuff. He was a real good guy. Those first two years, it was Art Gleason and I who did the games. It was terrific working with Art. He was a great guy and knew his baseball.

Just before that first season started, the San Francisco Giants were in spring training here. All the New York writers had come out because of that. I had gone to Homer Lane, who later became general manager and the top guy in both radio and TV for Tom Chauncey, and told him, "We should really broadcast the San Francisco Giants spring training games, because a lot of the players will wind up playing with the Phoenix Giants." He said, "That's fine. Let's go ahead and do it. Make your plans." I talked to the people at the big club, and they said, "Okay, no problem." About two weeks before the first exhibition game, I run into Homer Lane in the hall, and he says, "Oh, by the way, are you set to do those exhibition games?" I said, "Yes." He said, "We can't do them live during the week." "What do you mean?" I asked. "We've got too much CBS stuff. We'll do it live on Saturday and Sunday, but we'll have to play them back at night during the week. We'll play them back at eight o'clock."

Well, what am I going to do? It's two weeks before the first game. Four days before the game, I run into Homer Lane in the hall again. He said, "Oh, by the way, how long do those baseball games last?" I said, "It could be two-and-a-half hours. It could be three hours." Homer said, "They have to be done by 10, because *Richfield Reporter* is at 10 with a newscast, and we can't give that up. Make sure they're done by 10." With that, he walked off.

I didn't know how I was going to do this, but I wasn't going to give it up. I'm not going to say we're not going to do these games. I've already told all the San Francisco Giants people that we're going to do the games. I'd told Russ Hodges and Lon Simmons, who broadcast for the big club, that we were going to do the games.

One of the KOOL engineers was Joe Grahn, from Boston, and I told him, "Joe, here's what we're going to do. I want you to bring out to the ball park your big reel-to-reel tape recorder. I'm going to have a stopwatch." I had figured out that every game was going to have to be about an hour and 39 minutes because of commercials at the end of innings, etc. "You're going to have the recorder. I'm going to have a stopwatch. Every game is going to be an hour and 39 minutes." He asked me how I was going to do that. I said, "I'll tell you when to stop the tape, and I'll tell you when to start it." I started the broadcast, and if it looked like the inning was going to go long, I'd tell him to stop the tape. I'd stop my stopwatch. When the inning was over, I'd come on, start the stopwatch, recreate what had happened, and go on. Every one of those games I came in within **TIME***.

The funny part of that story is that a lot of the New York writers—one was Arch Murray—many times would have had a rough night and wouldn't get to the ball park until maybe the second or third inning. As I said, in that old ball park, there was just one area for the press. They'd get in the habit of coming over and looking at my scorecard to see what had happened the first few innings. When they walked over, I might be recreating the last inning. They could not figure out what the heck was going on. They thought I had the bad night! I had made up my mind that we were going to get those games in—and we did!

That year, when the exhibition season was over, the Giants went over to San Diego, which wasn't in the major leagues then, to play the Cleveland Indians there for a couple of games. Then they met up with the Dodgers and played in Fresno, Bakersfield,

*TIME of advertising breaks: 2 minutes and five seconds in the regular season, except on nationally televised games when you add 20 seconds; post season=2:55. Starting times are influenced by the fact that half of the U.S. population live in the Eastern Time zone.

and Sacramento. I went and did those games. Russ Hodges and Lon Simmons did those games for San Francisco. Jerry Doggett and Vin Scully did them for the Dodgers. That was when I first met Vin Scully, because we spent a lot of time together. Vin was just as great then as he is today. He's a really nice guy, and what a terrific broadcaster.

There was a lot of excitement in Phoenix about AAA baseball coming to town. They had a big booster club. It was the biggest thing that had happened to Phoenix. It was almost as big a deal as the Diamondbacks coming in 1998. Then, after two years in Phoenix, the team moved to Tacoma. While the team was in Tacoma, Phoenix finally built a new ball park. I did not go to Tacoma. When the city built the new ball park, the team came back to Phoenix in 1966.

In that first year, I interviewed Giants outfielder Dusty Rhodes and asked him, "James, where did you get that nickname?" He said, "Down in Alabama where I come from, you've got two choices—you're going to be called 'Dusty' or 'Muddy.' I didn't want to be called 'Muddy,' so they called me 'Dusty.'"

In that era, a lot of former major league players came down to play AAA in the later stages of their careers, for the money and to keep playing. Dusty Rhodes, Joey Amalfitano, Leon Wagner ("Daddy Wags"), Jack Dittmer (who had played at Iowa when I was still in the area) and **FELIPE ALOU*** were all on that team. Also, Willie McCovey came up late in the year. These were all good guys. I've always been a players' guy. No matter what sport I covered, I'd build good relationships with the players. They knew I wouldn't rip them. I'm going to be fair.

Graffiti seen in a Nebraska truck stop, 1973:
(Written on wall) The answer is Jesus.

(Written below)   What is the question?

(Written below)   The question is: What is the
                  name of **FELIPE ALOU**'s brother?

When I was doing the Phoenix Giants games the second time, when they were in the new ballpark on East Van Buren, I really got to know Horace Stoneham quite well. Horace's family had owned the New York Giants and moved them in 1958 to San Francisco. His whole life was baseball. He was a very gentle, unassuming man who loved his players and loved the game. He had a home in Phoenix so he would be in Phoenix a great deal during the baseball season. When the big club, San Francisco, was on the road, he'd come to his home in Phoenix and would come out to see the Phoenix Giants. He'd always pop into the booth to say 'hi.' We'd talk.

One night, he was at the ballpark, and he sent me a note which said, "Meet me in Rosy Ryan's office after the game." The fellow working with me at that time on the broadcast was Jack Beveridge, who had done a lot of radio and TV. He was a great baseball guy. When the game was over, we went down. Horace was already there and they were having a few nightcaps. It was going to be a longer night. Horace was the type individual who liked to have a good time and liked to have people with him. I couldn't blame him for that. We decided to leave the ballpark and go to the Pink Pony, owned by Charlie Briley, who had the club for years and was a great, great baseball fan and a friend of Horace's. So, now we are at the Pink Pony in Scottsdale until closing time. From there, we were off to Horace's house in Scottsdale. During the course of the evening, talking baseball, Horace turned to me and said, "I know you're going to be the next voice of the San Francisco Giants." He took out a napkin and started to draw up a contract. "How much money do you want? What do you want? Sign here. You're going to be the next voice of the Giants."

He was a very loyal individual and, as it turned out, through the years, I did have two opportunities to go to San Francisco to do the Giant games. Unfortunately, by that time, Horace had sold the club. They changed radio stations and were now on the NBC station, KNBR, and the general manager was a long-time friend of mine. We knew each other, and he respected my ability. The first time I was offered the job there was new ownership—Horace Stoneham was out. Things were shaky in San Francisco. They were talking about moving—wanting a new ballpark, and I just didn't feel that was going to be the right fit.

The second time I was offered the job, I was still doing the Suns. I really considered it. I was going to do both and then make a decision. As it turned out, I decided to stay in Phoenix...and I'm very glad that I did.

However, one year, their new announcers in San Francisco were Wayne Hagin and Ron Fairly. It was their first year together. As they were finishing up their exhibition season, Wayne Hagin had an emergency appendectomy. My friend, who was the general manager at KNBR in San Francisco, called me and said "Al, could you do a couple of Giant baseball games?" He told me what had transpired. It just so happened that it was in between Suns games. I did broadcast on KNBR a Giant game with Ron Fairly. By the way, we got pretty good reviews in the San Francisco press. So, although I was offered the job twice and didn't take it, I still wound up doing one of their games on KNBR in San Francisco and working with Ron Fairly.

I would see Horace Stoneham after that occasionally, and he would always kid me because I was doing the Suns games. He'd say, "Oh, you're with that sport where they change the rules every week." Meaning, of course, basketball and the NBA.

One of the things I get a nice feeling about—Horace passed away here in Phoenix, and I went to his services. When I was walking out of his funeral, Wes Westrum and Whitey Lockman were walking out and both turned to me and said, "When we visited the old man (meaning Horace, their boss), he always said, "Turn on Al McCoy so I can hear him." I had never met his wife. I met her at the funeral and she told me, "I just want you to know Horace thought so much of you." That meant a lot to me because I thought a lot of Horace. I appreciated the great love he had for the game. I always loved owners who loved the game, and Horace Stoneham certainly was that.

I kept busy during the off-season of my first stint at KOOL, after doing Phoenix Giants baseball. I did sports on TV and was program director at one time. This was before radio talk shows. In Los Angeles, the CBS station KNX did have a talk show called *Opinion Please*. It was sponsored by a vitamin company, and the host did not have opinions; he just took calls on the phone. When a call came in, he'd say, "You're on KNX, your opinion please."

Since KOOL was also a CBS station, the vitamin company wanted to buy an hour talk show in the evening on KOOL. The sales manager at KOOL came to me, since I was the program director at the time, and said, "Al, would you do this show? There's a talent fee, and it'll be on from eight to nine o'clock at night." I said, "Yeah, I need the money. I'll do it."

We started doing the show, and it was going along very well—we had a good audience with a lot of phone calls. This was during a period when the savings and loan business was under a lot of heat in Phoenix. One day, I came in to work, and the receptionist told me to go see Mr. Chauncey right away.

Unfortunately, some of the things on that show did not set well with Mr. Tom Chauncey, who was the top dog at KOOL radio and TV. It was during a period when savings and loan companies were taking a lot of heat. Mr. Chauncey had some friends in that business who were being raked over the coals on the show. He called me in and was very upset about that and was also was very upset I was getting a few dollars talent fee—he didn't like that. I guess, in my younger days, I made quick decisions also because I said, "Well, I guess if I'm working for someone who is concerned about how much money I'm making, I may be at the wrong place. Thank you, and goodbye."

I walked out of his office, went in the other room, and picked up the phone. I called a guy named George Lazley, the general manager of KRUX radio, a guy I used to occasionally run into, who was originally from **MINNESOTA***. He'd always jokingly say, "Hey, when are you going to come to work for me, Al?" We'd laugh about it. After this altercation with Tom Chauncey, I said to George, "Remember when I saw you last week, and you asked me when I was going to go to work for you? How about tomorrow?" He said, "Are you kidding?" I said, "No." He said, "Come and see me." Two weeks later I was on the air at KRUX.

In the first five years I was at KRUX, we were the "KRUX Good Guys." I was on from nine to noon. This was in the 1960s, and stations played a big variety of music. This was right before the Beatles came. When they came, we were on top of that, but you would also hear **FRANK SINATRA***, Dean Martin, maybe even the Beach Boys. It was a big mix, so it was really family radio. The promotions we did in those days were a lot of fun.

One of the best promotions I remember at KRUX was when Yamaha came out with a small motorcycle. They bought us all white jumpsuits with the KRUX logo and our names on the back. At ten o'clock one morning, all the on-air disc jockeys started on Central Avenue in Sunnyslope with a Yamaha. Everybody filled up with the same amount of gasoline. The contest involved driving these motorcycles only on Central Avenue from the top of Sunnyslope all the way down to South Mountain and back. The disc jockey whose Yamaha ran the longest was the winner. At the

---

*In 2009, during a promotion called "Reading to Succeed Night", the **MINNESOTA** Timberwolves handed out posters with "Timberwolves" misspelled…"Timberwoves."

---

*When Bobby Thomson hit "The Shot Heard Around the World" in 1951, Frank Sinatra and Jackie Gleason were at the game. When Thomson homered off Ralph Branca, Dodger fan Gleason did a technicolor yawn (vomited) on Sinatra's shoes…In the late '60s during an Old-Timers day at Shea Stadium, Thomson hit a Ralph Branca pitch into the left field bullpen…In the movie *The Godfather*, Sonny Corleone died while listening to that game…Dave Winfield was born that day.

same time, KRUX had a mobile unit—provided by Sanderson Ford—that followed us and did live on-air reports as to how it was all going.

By noon, interest was starting to pick up. By two or three o'clock, when the high schools started to let out, everything started to happen. Every kid in Phoenix with a car headed for Central Avenue. There was a well-known Bob's Big Boy restaurant at Central and Thomas at that time. By 3:30 p.m., their parking lot was jammed and Central was bumper to bumper. Our local police arrived on the scene, and that was the end of the promotion. But what fun!

By this time, in 1966, the new ball park was built. People were excited about the city fulfilling its commitment to build it and happy that it was finally completed. There was a six-year period of not having baseball in Phoenix, but in the interim period, I had done some Arizona State University football and basketball. I started doing that at KOOL, and then I flipped the ASU football package to KRUX when I went over there.

When I first came to Phoenix, Arizona State was not what it is today. They were in the Border Conference for football and basketball. I'll never forget the first year I was here. The high school tournament was to be played on ASU's campus at Sun Devil Gym. They didn't have the arena yet. I told my wife we should get over there early 'cause I didn't have tickets. Coming from Iowa, I expected it to be sold out. We got over there an hour before game time, and the gym was still locked up! When we went in, there were 200 people there.

The ASU basketball coach was Ned Wulk. I had met Ned when I was in Buffalo, and he was at Xavier, and they played in the Queen City Invitational in Buffalo. No one was broadcasting ASU games in '59, so I went to Ned and told him we needed to pick up some of their games. I talked to KOOL, and we started doing some of the ASU basketball games. Ned did a great job as the ASU coach and had a good recruiter working for him. The basketball program really started to zoom up.

At that time, the football broadcast rights seemed to jump around a lot between stations. When we got them on KOOL, I did the football games. The athletic director was Clyde Smith, and he suggested that we use Ned Wulk as the color guy, which we did. It was a great era at ASU. Frank Kush was the head football coach, Bobby Winkles was the baseball coach, and Baldy Castillo coached track. Those four guys did more to move ASU sports up into the big time than anybody.

When I started doing ASU basketball, they played in Sun Devil Gym, which held only a couple of thousand people. We'd go to New Mexico State and other Border Conference schools like Texas Western. Before the football team played at Sun Devil Stadium, there was another football field on campus, Goodwin Stadium, that probably held 20,000.

When I left KOOL, we met with ASU football, and they switched over to KRUX, because they wanted me to do the games. That was a big shock, because KRUX was a personality music station and not as powerful as KOOL or KTAR. Bob Zimmerman, who was an Iowa guy and had done sports there, was my color announcer for that year I did ASU football on KRUX.

The Frank Kush era just kept getting better every year. He was a winner, and I felt he was pushing ASU football toward the big time. He was able to recruit guys who could compete and play. They started winning consistently and were on their way up. Eventually ASU went into the Western Athletic Conference, a definite move up. After that, they joined the Pac-10. But it was a big deal for them when they went into the WAC.

Frank Kush was so successful because he worked harder than anybody and was a no-nonsense coach. When the players saw how he approached the game, he had the ability to make his players give 110 percent. He got the most out of them. With his background and his size, he was a survivor that had to be tough. Kush was a winner, no question about it. He did more for ASU than you can imagine.

Many years later, I'm with the Phoenix Suns. ASU has been through many athletic directors and coaches. They've just hired Herb Sendek to be their head basketball coach. I happened to be speaking at a luncheon, and the athletic director at Arizona State, Lisa Love, was there. I had not had the opportunity to meet her. She told me at the luncheon that she would like to talk to me. The next morning, she called me and asked if I had met Herb Sendek, the new basketball coach. I said, "No, I haven't. I just know him by reputation." She said, "Next week, I've invited 50 of the top business people in Phoenix to a luncheon at the Biltmore to meet Herb Sendek. Obviously, I will try to get them involved financially and other ways with ASU basketball. Would you be willing to come and either emcee or speak?" I chuckled and said, "I'm with the Phoenix Suns. We're the pro team." She said, "I know that, but I also know your background and how long you've been in Phoenix and how long you've been involved in basketball, going back to ASU. I would really appreciate it if you would feel comfortable doing it." I said, "I'd better check with my people before I give you an answer." She said, "I can understand that." I checked with our people, and they told me to go ahead if I wanted to do it.

The following week I show up at the luncheon at the Biltmore, which had a good turnout. They hand me a program, which read, "The featured speakers today: Lisa Love, athletic director; Al McCoy, voice of the Suns; Herb Sendek, basketball coach." So now I sit down at the head table with Herb Sendek and his wife and meet him for the first time. Lisa gets up and welcomes the people and tells them a little bit about things going on in the ASU basketball world. Then she introduces me.

Very briefly, I told them about the basketball history since I'd been here. I started with going to the high school tournament when the door was still locked an hour before the first game. I told them what Ned Wulk had done, how they had big tournament wins and how things had really developed at ASU during that era, and talked about the players they'd had. Then, I said the Suns had come to town in 1968, and we've had sellout crowds.

We've been in the Finals twice. This is a great basketball area. I said, "You people are ASU fans, and if we want to see ASU basketball up where it belongs, you have to get involved, not only with your support, but by helping out in many other ways. You now have a coach here who certainly has the background to put ASU where they belong in the basketball world. If you want to go along for the ride, you'd better get involved." Well, Herb wrote me a letter and said, "What can I say? I can't thank you enough for what you did." Also, Lisa Love was very appreciative.

They did not have a practice facility. I know that Robert Sarver, the owner of the Suns, contacted Coach Sendek and offered the Suns' practice facility for their use since they didn't have one. Coach Sendek was very appreciative, but he was concerned that the NCAA might frown upon a collegiate team working out on a pro team's practice facility.

Back in the '60s, while I was at KRUX, I broadcast some boxing and wrestling. In order to make a lot of money, you had to do a lot of different stuff. My first two years with the Suns I still did ASU football on TV, as a replay, not a live broadcast. When I was at KRUX, I did sports on Channel 3 and the wrestling on Channel 12. My deal with KRUX was such that I could do other things.

I was the boxing ring announcer at old Phoenix **MADISON SQUARE GARDEN***, on 7th Street just north of Van Buren in downtown. It was an old two-story boxing and wrestling arena. There were some great fighters there—Manny Elias was a ranked bantam weight, Jimmy Martinez was a ranked middleweight, and Zora Folley was a ranked heavyweight. They packed that little arena, which could probably hold 1,200. The place was raucous. I had to give it up, because I was getting so much blood on my sportscoats and ties that my wife was complaining. I was right there at ringside. That was quite an era for boxing here in Phoenix.

***BOSTON GARDEN** was originally named Boston Madison Square Garden.

The boxing promoter's name was Paul Clinite, and he had the cigar and the hat, just like Knobby Walsh in the old Joe Palooka cartoon. He promoted boxing in Texas, too. He was a boxing character, that's for sure, and he definitely made money. Many times, I'd get in the ring to interview a fighter with blood on my clothes.

I remember one in particular. He was a really outstanding welterweight and middleweight, and I got in the ring and said, "How you doing? I haven't seen you in a while. Where have you been?" "I was down in Florence for six or eight months, but I'm back. I'm in great shape." Florence is the location of the state prison.

I liked all sports. As a kid, I listened to Don Dunphy, the best at doing **BOXING***. I was always a boxing fan. When Zora Folley was the heavyweight contender, the Caravan Inn had just been built on East Van Buren. It was the plush motel in the area. *Friday Night Fights* was on ABC at that time. They constructed a ring over the swimming pool. They had a nationally televised fight in Phoenix between Zora Folley and Alonzo Johnson. Bill Swift managed Zora Folley then. Jack Drees did that fight, and I was the ring announcer. Drees was an Iowa guy who had done Big 10 sports and was then a network announcer.

It was a big week in Phoenix promoting the fight. Everybody was in town, including all the networks. The referee for the main event was Max Baer. Max had been here all week, and there had been a lot of parties and get-togethers. The night before the main event, I'm up in the ring getting ready to introduce the fighters. Max was over in the corner. I walked over to him and said, "Hi, Max. How you doing?" He said, "I'm not feeling too good tonight. I'm a little under the weather. I may be getting the flu." He refereed the main event. He left that night for California after the fight. The next morning, he was shaving and had a heart attack and died.

***PETE ROSE** is enshrined in the Summit County (Ohio) Boxing Hall of Fame.

Zora Folley was from here in Chandler. He was a wonderful, great guy, but just couldn't get fights in those days. He was excellent, a top contender, and could very well have been a champion, but he couldn't get fights. He didn't get a title fight until very late in his career. When he fought Cassius Clay, Zora was way beyond his prime.

When Cassius Clay came to Phoenix before his one fight in Las Vegas, it was the first time I had met him, and I got him for an interview. We did the interview live and in rhyme! We started just as a gag and wondered how long we could keep it up. We went on at least three or four minutes. He had no preparation at all. That's pretty hard to do. Of all the fighters I interviewed over the years, **MUHAMMAD ALI*** is certainly at the top.

When you do TV, you get the opportunity to do lots of different things. I had the chance to do some Roller Derby on Channel 5 here in Phoenix. At one point, Roller Derby matches were held here outdoors. Matches were also held at the Coliseum. That was back in the '60s. When I was at KRUX, I was doing a lot of free-lance work, so I did Roller Derby for about a year. Announcing it is almost like wrestling. It's all make believe, but they put on a great show, and the fans really get involved.

The San Francisco Bay Bombers were a popular Roller Derby team. Their superstar was a very tall buxom blond who had polka dots in her hair. She just recently passed away, and there was an article in *Sports Illustrated* on her. My first meeting with her was when they were in the Coliseum in the early days. We were shooting it for TV, and I wanted to talk with her before the match. When she came in, she said, "Come on, just follow me." Well, I followed her right into the locker room where all the lady teams were dressing. They were in panties and bras and Shirley changed while I was talking to her. If it didn't bother her, it didn't

---

*Rich Kotite, former head coach of the Eagles and the Jets, was once **MUHAMMAD ALI**'s sparring partner in Miami.

bother me. I got everything I needed and walked out. Show business is my life!

In the mid-sixties, when I had come back to KOOL radio and TV, the most exciting thing happening in Phoenix was that they were getting a professional hockey team. At that time, there were only eight teams in the National Hockey League. The Western Hockey League in the West and the American Hockey League in the East were almost like AAA baseball teams; they were just a skate under the NHL. At this time, the Victoria BC hockey team, which was a farm club of the Toronto Maple Leafs, moved to Phoenix. That was 1967.

The original general manager was Bob Whitlow, who'd had various sports jobs, including with the **AIR FORCE ACADEMY*** and the Chicago Cubs. They brought in a sportscaster I had known in Buffalo, Jim Wells, who had been in sales in Phoenix but had a love of hockey. He was hired by the Roadrunners as their public relations director and broadcaster. They eventually worked out deals for KOOL radio to broadcast their games and Channel 5 to do some of their games on TV.

I had been doing the Phoenix Giants in the summer, but since this was a winter sport, and I happened to know Jim Wells, he asked me if I would work with him on the hockey games. I told him I didn't know much about hockey. The first time I was exposed to hockey, I was growing up on a farm in Iowa and doing my usual Saturday night search for all the sporting event radio broadcasts I could find. I dialed up a program and heard the announcer saying, "And he shoots, it's off the net, he rebounds, and he scores." I thought it was a basketball game. It was Foster Hewitt broadcasting Toronto Maple Leafs hockey.

---

*Bill Parcells was head coach at the **AIR FORCE ACADEMY** in 1978. His record was 3-8.

I asked Jim what I could do. He told me I could do pregame, fill in between periods, and do some interviews. That first year, Jim Wells did the play-by-play, and I worked with him on color.

The Roadrunners' second season in Phoenix had just gotten underway. We were waiting at the airport in Phoenix to go to Denver for a game. I noticed Jim Wells had not arrived. All of a sudden, here comes Bob Whitlow, the general manager, running into the airport. He came up to me and said, "Al, you're gonna have to do the game." I said, "What's the matter?" It turned out that Jim Wells had fallen through a glass shower door, and had it not been for the fact that his wife was an RN, he would have had a really tough time. He was hospitalized immediately.

I thought, "Oh boy, here we go. I'm going to get a hockey lesson in a hurry." The writer covering the Roadrunners for the *Phoenix Gazette* was a Canadian named Doug McConnell. He was born and bred in hockey, so on the flight up I asked him if he would sit with me. He knew what had happened and that I was going to have to do the game. He said he would. That game against the Denver team was the first hockey play-by-play I had ever done.

I guess maybe the good part is it's a similar broadcast to basketball. It's a fast-paced game, up and down. As I continued on, the more I did it, the more I enjoyed it. It was almost six weeks before Jim Wells was well enough to come back. When he did, he said, "Al, why don't you continue to do the play-by-play, and I'll just do the color." I got to really enjoy hockey and the players.

There was a young man named Mike Lange who had just graduated from college. He came down to Phoenix to interview for a broadcasting job. We talked, and he was a very nice, personable young guy. He had a real love for hockey, and his only goal in life was to be a hockey announcer. We didn't have anything with the Roadrunners, so he went all over the country looking for a job. Finally, at the end of the summer, just before the hockey season was starting, he shows up back in Phoenix. He came to me and said he couldn't find anything and didn't know what he was going to do. I told him, "Mike, if you want to hang around, get yourself a room here. I can't promise you'll make a lot of money, but I think I could get the club to hire you on an hourly basis. I'll do what I can for you." He started by helping me out with statistics and other things.

As luck would have it, just a few weeks later, Moon Mullins, the guy who had become the PR guy for the Roadrunners and had been at Arizona State University for a number of years before taking the PR job here, was offered the PR job with the Denver Broncos. He couldn't turn that down. I went to Roadrunner management and said, "Why don't you hire Mike Lange to do PR? He's here with us, and he'd do a great job." Since they were in this jam with Moon Mullins leaving after the start of the season, they hired Mike Lange.

I slowly began to work him into our broadcast more and more. He did interviews and the pregame show. He became a great friend and started to become a real contributor to the broadcast. When I left to join the Suns in 1972, I suggested that Mike Lange take over the play-by-play job—and he did. When the '74 season proved to be the end for the Roadrunners because the World Hockey Association was coming in, Mike was able to get the World Hockey Association job in San Diego. That league did not last very long. Following that, Mike nabbed the Pittsburgh Penguins job, where he's been their voice for many years. He was named to the Hockey Broadcasters Hall of Fame. He's a great friend and has had a great career.

Hockey players are a great group of guys, and they all love to play the game. A majority of them through the years have been from Canada and have grown up with the game. The first thing to hit me with hockey players was that they could have injuries, they could have cuts, and they'd want to hide it from the coach. I remember doing an interview after a game with a player who had tremendous cuts above and on the side of his eye. The first thing he said to me was, "Don't tell the coach. Don't tell the coach." He was afraid he wouldn't be able to play.

Vancouver always was one of the top teams in the Western Hockey League. This particular season, they had quite a winning streak on their home ice. The Roadrunners went there to play them and, wouldn't you know, they wound up breaking the Vancouver Canucks' long winning streak .

In the locker room after the game, several of the players said, "Al McCoy, you're going out with us tonight. We've got a friend here we want you to meet." There was a nightclub at Vancouver called either "the Cove" or "the Cave." It was a very nice place with good entertainment, so about 10 of the players and I go to this club. They knew the guy who was appearing there and invited him over to our table. He was from Canada and was a huge hockey fan.

They introduced me to him, and his name was Rich Little, at that time an unknown talent. I guess he knew all the hockey players in Canada. They were kidding him and, after he met me, we were all talking, and he was getting ready to leave us. They knew that, at one point in his act, he would ask for people to call out names so he could imitate them. One of the players said, "Hey, you'd better know how to imitate Al McCoy," and everybody laughed.

Rich Little goes up to do his act. When he gets to the point in his show where he asks people in the crowd to call out names for him to impersonate, one of our players said, "Okay, Al McCoy." Everyone at our table laughed, and he did an Al McCoy impersonation. Unfortunately, *shazam* wasn't around then. I seem to remember him saying, "...and he scores!"

Later that night, I left the club and went back to our hotel, the Georgian Towers. It had been an apartment house during the war, so the rooms were all mini apartments and had doorbells. It was after one o'clock in the morning, and I had just gotten in bed. I hear guys coming down the hall and have a pretty good idea who's making this noise. Then I hear doorbells starting to ring, including my own. I get up and open the door, leaving the security chain on. Here are some of the Roadrunners. I said,

"Hey, you guys better hold it down or somebody's gonna make a phone call, and there will be all kinds of problems on this floor."

Millie Marcetta said, "I'm going to come in your room. I'm the captain of the team. You guys go to bed." I let him in. We sat down, and he pulled a bottle of wine out of his pocket and wanted to pour me a glass. I'm trying to get him calmed down, saying, "We had a big win tonight, but it's time to shut it down." We were on the tenth floor of the hotel. Our phone rang, and I told Millie to pick it up. It was one of the other players, and he wanted to come in and join our little party. Millie said, "No, you guys get out of here. I'm the captain. I'm here with Al. You guys get to bed." He hangs up.

I look over toward the window of my hotel room and all of a sudden I see an arm, and a hand starts tapping on my window. The ledge outside that window was *maybe* about 12 inches wide! I look up, and here is one of our players knocking on the window and yelling, "Hey you guys, let me in. Let me in." I visualized the headline in the newspaper: "Hockey Player Falls from Sportscaster's Room." The good news is that Millie looked up to this player—who shall remain nameless—and waved him away. How that guy crawled back on that ledge to get to his room, I'll never know.

Mike Leonard has been a popular figure on the *Today Show* for almost twenty years. Several years ago, he wrote a bestselling book called *The Ride of Our Lives* about taking his mom and dad around America in rented RVs visiting their old haunts. It also became a hit on PBS in documentary form, but years ago Mike's heart was broken when the Roadrunners cut him.

Mike Leonard was a tremendous guy who loved hockey; he played in college and did sports on TV. He would remember three of the great guys on that team that we called "the go-go line." Larry Lund was at center ice, and Andy Hines and Frankie Hughes were the two wings. They were one of the most exciting lines in the Western Hockey League. Andy Hines was a little Frenchman who was as tough as you could be. He could get in front of that net, and they'd have to knock him down and tie him up to get him out. The go-go line was very popular around the league.

I knew Mike's family originally through his dad, Jack Leonard. Jack was out of Chicago and had been with *Sports Illustrated* when the magazine started. He later moved to Phoenix and even sponsored some of my sports shows. He was also a hockey fan and gave me some great tips when I started doing the games full time when I took over from Jim Wells. He was a big help to me. Mike became a sportscaster in Phoenix and even had his own little store that sold all kinds of hockey equipment. He was a genuine hockey guy.

After being with the Roadrunners for five years, I started with the Suns. When I did speaking engagements, I'd always get asked, "What's the difference, Al, between players in the NBA and hockey players?" My standard answer was, "Sometimes after a big game at home, maybe while still in the Suns locker room, one of the guys will say, 'Why don't I grab a case of beer, and you guys come on over, and we'll have some sandwiches and a beer at my house?'" I said, "If that was a hockey locker room, they'd probably say, 'Listen you guys, let's each get a case of beer and come over to my house.'" But they were great guys and competitors, and I really learned to love the game of hockey. That was a very good hockey league.

The first two years the Suns were in Phoenix, the Roadrunners had bigger crowds. They made the playoffs and were a very exciting team. That's why I've always felt there is a future for hockey in Phoenix.

There are a lot of hockey fights. Millie Marcetta had played in the National Hockey League for a number of years, and then, in the later years of his career, played for quite a while with Phoenix. In one of the Roadrunner games in Colorado, we were playing the Denver Spurs out at the Broadmoor, a big resort in Colorado Springs that has a nice ice arena. Back in the sixties, no one wore helmets, and the goalies didn't wear face masks. There was only one player I can remember who wore a helmet in the league.

Millie was defending the net. An opposing player fired a slap shot from the point that caromed up and hit him right in the forehead. It split his forehead, and he went down on the ice. They had to come out and take him off the ice on a stretcher. This happened in the second period. I was trying to get a report on his condition to see how he was doing. What I learned was, "They're taking a lot of stitches, and he was knocked out." Then I finally heard that they were going to wait until we got back to Phoenix, but he's out on the dressing room table with ice on his head.

After the game was over, I go down to the locker room and get ready for all of us to get on a bus back to the hotel. We were flying back to Phoenix the next morning. Sandy Hucul was the coach. He'd been a great defenseman with the Roadrunners and was a wonderful person. Believe it or not, there was no Millie Marcetta. He's gone. Where do you think Millie is? Well, we all get on the bus. A couple of the players suggest checking a few of the little bars in the area. Sandy was upset. We find the first bar and send in a couple of the players. They come out and report he isn't there. We go to the next bar, another guy goes in, and time goes by. He comes out with Marcetta. Millie got on the bus, and his forehead's all taped up. He gets back to where I'm sitting, and I say to him, "Hey Millie, what's going on? How you doing in there?" He said, "Hey, it's not bad having double vision. Order one beer, you get two!"

When the World Hockey Association started, it unfortunately spelled the end of the Western Hockey League. The Western Hockey League, at the top of its popularity, just didn't have the right leadership. It was a terrific league. San Diego, Denver, Vancouver, Portland, and Seattle all drew huge crowds and had a big following. But they didn't fight to retain their popularity when the World Hockey Association came in.

The Roadrunners went to Denver for a playoff game and eliminated them. After the game at the hotel, I'm on the same floor with a lot of the players. It was relatively quiet. About two o'clock in the morning, there was a knock at my room door. I was asleep, but I get up and go to the door. Here are several of the hockey players in their shorts. They had a serving cart like the ones used for room service. The only difference was that they had a young lady who was completely disrobed, and they wanted to wheel her into my room. Fortunately, being the man that I am, I put the lock back on the door.

I was very familiar with the Coliseum, and when there were a couple of NBA preseason games scheduled there, that's when I really made my inroads for an NBA job with the Suns. There hadn't been any buzz about the NBA coming to Phoenix. I was working at KRUX, and after the Phoenix Giants came back in 1966, I went back to KOOL in order to do the games. Shortly after I was back at KOOL, there was an NBA preseason game played at the Coliseum between the St. Louis Hawks and Philadelphia Warriors.

I had talked KOOL into carrying the Lakers games with **CHICK HEARN***, whom I had known from my Midwest days. When I was at Drake, working at a local radio station in Des Moines, doing some of the basketball games, Chick Hearn was doing the Bradley University games from Peoria, Illinois. When he walked into the Drake Fieldhouse to do the Bradley-Drake game, I met him. I thought, "Boy, that's the job I want." Chick was a great-looking guy, a sharp dresser, and we became great friends. Years later, he winds up in L.A. with the Lakers, and I wind up in Phoenix with the Suns. We often joked about those Missouri Valley Conference days.

---

*In late 1953 the St. Louis baseball Cardinals chose Jack Buck for play-by-play over CHICK HEARN from Peoria, Illinois. Buck got the job because he had done excellent Budweiser commercials that summer while broadcasting the Rochester Red Wings, the Cardinals' AAA team in New York. The Cardinals had just been purchased by Anheuser-Busch.

One of my great remembrances was in my 30th year with the Suns. We were playing the **LAKERS***, and the Suns set up a little presentation for me. They wanted to have a luncheon with Chick and me with the media. Chick, at this point, was having some health problems and wasn't prone to doing that type of thing the day of a game. But when he found out about it, he called me and said, "Hey, Al, whatever you want, I'll do anything for you." I told him we would send a car to pick him up. We had the luncheon at the arena in one of the clubs. Chick and I sat on stools and just talked, going back to our days in Illinois and Iowa and on to the NBA. I have a picture of the two of us from that day. As far as I know, nobody recorded that luncheon, but it was a day I will never forget!

Chick and I did a couple of NBA All-Star Games together on national radio. I still have the introduction he gave me on tape. I thought he was introducing somebody else it was so flowery. As I've always said, Chick Hearn in the West and Marty Glickman in the East are the two guys who really set the stage for broadcasting basketball. They blazed the trail, and the rest of us have just followed. When I gave my acceptance speech at the Basketball Hall of Fame, I said exactly that.

After Chick passed away, one of my great memories came the next year when I was in Los Angeles to do a Suns-Lakers game. One of the broadcast engineers I've known for years told me that Chick's wife, Marge, was at the game and would like to see me. As we walked toward each other, she put her arms around me and said, "I just want you to know how much Chick loved you." It doesn't get any better than that.

*In March 1954, the **LAKERS** and the Hawks played a regulation, regular season NBA game using baskets that were 12' high rather than the usual 10'...the next night they played each other in a doubleheader. True facts, believe it or not!

HOCKEY WOULD BE MORE FUN IF THE PUCK WAS TRANSPARENT

Mike Lange

Mike Lange is in his 34th year as the play-by-play voice of the Pittsburgh Penguins. In 2001, he received the Foster Hewitt Memorial Award for his outstanding work as an NHL broadcaster. A native of Sacramento, Lange joined the Penguins as a radio announcer in 1974 after spending time as a commentator for the San Diego Gulls and Phoenix Roadrunners of the Western Hockey League. His colorful and creative play-by-play calls are legendary in the NHL and frequently are carried on YouTube.

I grew up in Sacramento, went to school there, and was fortunate enough to have the opportunity to do some football, basketball, and baseball for one of the radio stations there. I ended up doing some hockey as well. I kept the hockey tapes, and I later sent them out along with a lot of baseball things I was doing. The only real feeler I got back as a possibility was in Phoenix, Arizona. I was spirited, young, and ready to roll, so I packed my bags and moved to Phoenix. The feelers were from a minor league hockey team called the Roadrunners. I thought, "I'm going to take a shot." I went to Phoenix without knowing anybody there. It was 1970, and I just went to work. I was able to find a place to stay for a decent amount and started walking over to the Roadrunners' offices every day asking if there was a job open, any job. I got turned down again and again, but as it turns out, I started looking for radio work in Phoenix, too. I knew that Al did the hockey games, but I had not met him. I called him, and he was receptive, just talking to me about where I was going. From that we built a kinship. I came in and did some mock games at the Veterans Coliseum. He helped get me a recorder and critiqued a few things. Lo and behold, I started doing some stats for him and ended up being his color man. I was hired by the Roadrunners as a PR and color guy. That's how it all began with Al and me.

I don't know why he took a shine to me. Obviously, it thrilled me! Maybe he saw the passion in me for broadcasting. From our end, a lot of people can talk the talk but very few have that deep passion. You can see it pretty early. He probably related to himself when he was younger. He just took me under his wing. I can't say enough about the things he taught me about broadcasting—the day-to-day operation, how to do a game, and what's important.

Phoenix was a very transient city for a young guy starting out. It still is somewhat the kind of place where people come in droves from a lot of different places to live. It was vibrant. It had a young demographic and a lot to offer, for me anyway. There were so many young people you could gravitate to. Having said that, I got a big break when Al decided to go over to the Suns. That was a huge opportunity for me to be able to move in and become a play-by-play guy.

Quite frankly, back in that era, both Phoenix and San Diego, just for your information, paid six million dollars to the NHL to be accepted in the league...even at that time! Gary Hooker paid that money in Phoenix, and Karl Eller was involved, too. Then the World Hockey Association came in, put franchises in those two cities, and effectively killed the Western Hockey League. So they moved right in. That's when the WHA started up.

Probably the best thing Al McCoy taught me when I first started was when he said to me, "Just stay in the background and keep your mouth shut. Just watch and listen." In those days, with a minor league hockey team, there were no charter flights when you finished a game, so we stayed overnight and would come back on commercial flights the next morning. After a game, we would go out and drink beers with the players and sit around. This was very early on, and I'm learning a lot of things about hockey.

We were sitting there one night, and there were three players talking about what happened at the game. I chimed in at a certain point, probably after about the fourth beer, and one of the players looked at me and said, "What do you know about hockey?" I just stopped in my tracks. I thought about Al McCoy and said to myself, "You know what? He's absolutely right. Just keep your mouth shut and listen." And I did for a lot of years. That's how I answered that guy. I didn't say a word. I knew he was right. It was one of those moments you say, "What do you know about hockey at this point in your life?" I just backed off, and it was a great learning process.

I never thought the NBA would ever come to my hometown of Sacramento. I certainly never envisioned Sacramento being as big as it is now. I never envisioned Phoenix being that big either. When I was in Phoenix, they were the 23rd largest market in the country, and when I went to Pittsburgh, Pittsburgh was number nine. Now it's just the opposite. I was in Phoenix for only two-and-a-half years.

Al is like a second father to me. Again, it's hard for me to emphasize how much he taught me and what he meant to me. He's been back here, and I've gone to see him when we're in Phoenix. He's brought his wife, Georgia, to **PITTSBURGH***. We've remained friends for a long time.

The ***PITTSBURGH PIRATES** was also the name of a National Hockey League team for five seasons in the 1920s.

Chapter 4

THE PHOENIX SUNS

Swisheroos & Shazams

S for Solomon's wisdom
H for Hercules' strength
A for Atlas' stamina
Z for Zeus' power
A for Achilles' great courage
M for Mercury's speed
That was Shazam!

(From *Captain Marvel, DC Comics*, 1940)

In **1966*** I heard there was an NBA exhibition game coming to Phoenix. I made a few calls, and I found out that the game would feature the St. Louis Hawks and the Philadelphia Warriors. I also found out that Marty Blake was the general manager of the St. Louis Hawks. I called him, and I said, "I know you have a game out here in a few weeks. Our station would like to broadcast the game." He said, "Aw, kid, we can't have the game broadcast. We're trying to sell tickets." I came back and said, "Well, now wait a minute! How 'bout if we give you a spot package to promote the game?" I had prepared how many spots a day we would give him over a two-week period. "And we won't even mention we are going to broadcast the game at all."

"You'll give me these spots? No charge?" he asked. I assured him, "No charge!" "Well, I might go for that!" he said. "Can I take care of the spots?" I said, "Sure! You've got a 30-second spot. You'll get so many each day for the two weeks prior, and we can broadcast the game live." He said, "Get that to me in writing, kid!" So, I did.

I did the game. We had a nice turnout. It was exciting. It was my first chance to broadcast a pro game. I loved it. That was a couple

---

* *Sports Illustrated* rated New York City circa **1966** as the worst time and place to be a sports fan. The Yankees, Knicks and Rangers finished last, the Mets escaped last place for the first time and the Giants were 1–12–1. The best time and place to be a sports fan? Philadelphia, 1980.

of years before the Suns, but I don't remember if that game sparked any talk about a possible NBA team in Phoenix. They might have been testing the market. It's hard to say.

As I remember, there were probably six or seven thousand people at the Coliseum, which was pretty new at the time. Exhibition games drew well in those days, because there wasn't all the TV coverage, and it was a big event for people to go see an NBA game.

I don't remember many details from that game, but I do remember what I did afterward. I don't think I've ever told Jerry Colangelo this story. I enlisted my good friend Chuck Clemens to help me. I'd started him in the business as a disc jockey in Phoenix. He later went on to California and had an outstanding career. Chuck was an expert with a razor blade, which was how you edited tape back in those days...cut and splice. I had the game recorded, obviously, because I wanted to keep it. Chuck and I went through the tape and edited it. We took out every pause and every mistake until we had about 10 minutes of the best play-by-play tape this side of Chick Hearn. Eventually, that was the tape I gave to Jerry Colangelo. It was well worth it to broadcast that game, because that's what eventually got me the job with the Suns. I still have that tape!

I had that NBA game under my belt, but then I left KOOL radio after doing the Phoenix Giants for about three seasons. I went back to KRUX radio and was on the air there. In the three years I was gone, a lot of the guys there had left, and their ratings had dropped. George Lazley was the general manager at KRUX and a friend of mine. He asked me if I would come back as station manager to try to get them back on track. I said I would do it for one year.

I was program director at a couple of stations. The program director handles the programming. He hires the announcers; he's in charge of programming and is basically in charge of the "sound" of the radio station. It's a tough job. My son, Mike, is also in the business and has been program manager for several years at Clear Channel station KJ103 in Oklahoma City. He's also worked in Pittsburgh and in various other markets. He loves it, but it's a tough, tough job.

A manager is more in charge of all of the things involved at the station. But basically, even as manager, my main focus was the sound of the station and the hiring of the announcers. I took that job in 1969 for one year. A lot of trust is put in the position and that of program director as well.

It was a tough year. I went through a lot of announcers, and I decided that I was done with management. I wanted to get back to doing sports and doing my own thing.

The buzz around town was that there might be an NBA team coming. The commissioner of the NBA at that time was Walter Kennedy. Kennedy came to Phoenix and asked the guy shining his shoes at the airport if he thought an NBA team would make it here. The guy said he thought it would. True story!

Three guys who had been friends at the University of Arizona, and were friends of the owners of the **SEATTLE*** Sonics, applied for an NBA franchise for Phoenix. I've told this story many times, but when the announcement of the new franchise came prior to the 1968 season, I don't think it was even on the front page of the sports section in Phoenix. It was not a big deal.

They hired Jerry Colangelo, and at age 28, he was the youngest general manager in all of pro sports. Johnny Kerr was announced as the head coach. I knew Johnny and his wife, Betsy, from my years in the Midwest, so when John came in for his press conference, he said, "Hey, you're going to do the games, aren't you?" I said, "Well, I haven't really talked to Jerry." He said, "Well, get with Jerry!" I got with Jerry, gave him my famous tape, and after

---

***During the SEATTLE Mariners' first year in 1977, the distance to the fences was measured in fathoms. A fathom is 6 feet. For instance, whereas one park might have a sign that denotes 360 feet, the Kingdome sign would have the number 60...**

listening to it and to a lot of other tapes, he said, "Boy, that's the best tape I've heard, and I've heard all kinds of announcers!" He didn't know that I doctored it up, though. He said, "I'd really like you to do the games. What do you think?" I said, "Jerry, it's time for a pro sports team to handle everything. Why sell your rights to a station? Why not bring it in-house and handle your own radio and TV? Do your own sales. Otherwise, you're just competing with yourself all the time."

Nobody was doing that at the time, really. Baseball was hiring their own announcers and starting to go that way. I thought with my background in programming, sales, and putting deals together that this would be a good option. I didn't want to go to another station. I didn't want to keep hopping around, and Jerry liked the idea. But in that first year, the fan interest wasn't that high, and season tickets were not selling as well as the owners thought they would. I thought the NBA would work here, but, of course, I'm a sports fan.

Karl Eller, at that time, owned KTAR **RADIO*** and KTAR television, Channel 12. Karl was initially going to be part of the ownership group, but decided not to get involved. Eller went to Colangelo, and, as I understand it, this is what happened: Karl said to Jerry, "I know that season ticket sales are not going that well, and you'd probably like to have some money in-house. Why don't I buy the radio and television rights for the first few years and give you some upfront money?" How is Jerry going to turn that deal down? Now Jerry and Karl both come back to me, and Jerry said, "Why don't you go to work for KTAR?" I talked with Karl and said that I just didn't think it was the right time. I said "If I'm going to make a move, I want it to be the right move. I'm still sold on the way it should be handled. I just don't want to go to another station. Who knows how long this deal will last?"

*The New York Yankees, Brooklyn Dodgers and New York (baseball) Giants banned **RADIO** coverage of their regular-season games between 1934 and 1938...fearing damage to their attendance.

I put in my year at KRUX, and the Suns, for that first year, used KTAR's sports director, Bob Vache, to broadcast the games. They had a small television package, maybe 10 or 12 games, and they were simulcast with Bob Vache. Bob was a terrific guy and had been in the market a long time. He'd done ASU sports and was a very solid broadcaster, but the Suns owners didn't really feel he did anything to create interest and excitement. They decided to bring in Hot Rod Hundley, who had been with the Lakers and Chick Hearn for several years.

The three major owners of the Suns were Don Pitt, Don Diamond (who both still live in Tucson), and Richard Bloch, who owned Filmways International. They had all attended U of A together. For additional investors in the Suns, they brought in a group of Hollywood people headed up by singer Andy Williams, who had a major piece. Also on the investor list were Bobbie Gentry, Ed Ames, Tony Curtis, Henry Mancini, and on down the line. Andy Williams stayed in for a long time. I used to kid him all the time that his hometown was smaller than mine. Andy was from Wall Lake, Iowa. He and his brothers started their singing careers at WHO radio in Des Moines. Tony Curtis was unbelievable. They'd have all these meetings, and he'd want to tell everyone how to run the team.

Don Diamond's wife was originally from Iowa. Her family owned Younkers, wonderful department stores. He was one of the good guys. Anyway, the Suns bring Hot Rod Hundley onto the broadcast team. By January of the second year, they had worked Bob Vache to death. When he was off the road and back here, he had to do TV and radio sports on KTAR, as well as some special engagements for the Suns. He was on his way home one night, missed a curve near Greyhound Park, hit a pole, and was killed.

Meanwhile, I was doing the Roadrunners, a minor league hockey team, on KPHO radio and on KPHO Channel 5, because I had started with the Roadrunners in the late '60s. When Bob was killed at about two o'clock in the morning, my phone rang at 4 a.m. It was Jerry Colangelo. He tells me what happened. He said, "Al, you've got to do the games." I said, "Jerry, I'm doing the hockey games. I can't do that!" So what does he do in the next 24 hours? He relieves Johnny Kerr of his coaching duties, and Colangelo takes over coaching the team himself. He then makes Johnny Kerr and Hot Rod the new Suns announcing team. Hot Rod had been the color commentator.

When Rod started doing play-by-play for the Suns, he didn't pace himself well, and he'd usually begin losing his voice by the third quarter. The classic story about Rod was a game in Atlanta that I happened to be listening to. They were playing the Hawks in a Sunday game at Georgia Tech. Hot Rod had a big night the night before. At halftime, he goes back into the locker room to get some aspirin and lies down. Well, he falls asleep in the trainers' room. The players leave and forget about him, and here's Rod's partner, Johnny Kerr, stuck. Kerr had to do the whole second half by himself....

Jerry comes to me when there was still another year left on the KTAR deal. Jerry was convinced, because I got it across to him, that all he's going to do is compete with KTAR. I told him, "Every time your salespeople go out to sell program ads and in-house deals and personal appearances, they're saying they bought the time from KTAR and that they are already with the Suns." Jerry was beginning to see the light. I said, "Jerry, when this contract is up, we'll get together." He said OK. So they hired Joe McConnell. Joe is a real good broadcaster, but he just had problems getting along with people. At the end of the season, that was it. Then Jerry and I got together.

It was the last year of the KTAR contract, and I decided to go ahead. I was employed both by the Suns and KTAR. That first year, I had an office at KTAR. I was taking the broadcast package in-house for the Suns and away from KTAR, but I had an office over at KTAR. Sometimes it is a strange business.

After that one year at KRUX, I went to another station here, KXIV, which was owned by the comedian Dick Van Dyke. I went there because I wanted to get back to doing sports. I was talking to

Jerry about the Suns. This was 1970. I went to Ira Lavin, who was the GM of the station. It was a good music station with great personalities. I went to Ira and said, "I want to do five sports shows a day." He said, "Can't sell them!" I said, "I'll sell them in two weeks!" And I did, one to a guy who had a horse ranch here, Jack Leonard.

I went to KXIV and ended up being program director there and now it's 1972. I talked Jerry Colangelo into bringing everything in-house. After the KTAR deal expired, KXIV carried the games, and then I got an FM station to also carry the games. It's now 92.3, KTAR-FM. Before I came in, the Suns did not have affiliates in Flagstaff and Tucson, so I set up the network, too.

Then we went to KOOL for the '75-'76 season. That was the only year we were on KOOL, because we went back to KTAR, and we've been there ever since. Of course, we simulcast, from day one, on radio and television. The Lakers had done it since they started, and other teams followed their lead. Few teams do it anymore, because they can produce more revenue by doing the broadcasts separately. Chick, Hot Rod, and I were the last three in the NBA to do simulcasts. I will put our simulcasts up to any of the television-only broadcasts.

When Bryan Colangelo got involved with the Suns organization, he wanted a younger approach on television. They decided to split and not simulcast. Rick Welts had also joined the organization. First, they were going to do it, and then they weren't going to do it. The Suns had contracts with Budweiser and other sponsors who were already getting ads on both radio and TV through the simulcast. How were you going to go back to them now and say we have to charge you more because it's separate? At virtually the last minute, about a month before the season, they decided to go with the split, because the league was pushing for it. Welts came to me and asked me what I wanted to do. I asked what he wanted me to do, and he said, "Well, right now, I don't know who we would get to do the radio. We've got Tom Leander already in-house, and we could slide him over to do TV." I said as long as it didn't cut me financially, I didn't care. So I did the radio.

When it was first taken in-house in 1972, it was Jerry Colangelo and me selling the Phoenix Suns. Jerry would call the president of the bank or the CEO of a company and say, "Can we have lunch with you?" Their advertising agency wouldn't be invited, and Jerry and I would go and have lunch with the decision maker. I would do the presentations at that time. We'd go in and sell the broadcast. If we were good enough, the president of that bank would call the advertising agency and tell the agency they were buying the Suns. The agencies would be upset, but that's how we did it. And it worked! Then I would produce the games. Since Jerry was running the franchise at that time, he could call the top guy of any business in town and get an appointment to make our presentation. At that time, we were only televising maybe 15 games. That number started going up over the years. We were on Channel 5 for awhile and then back to Channel 12. I had to do everything. They wouldn't send a director or producer on the road. I would go into a city like Chicago and hire a director and crew to do the game. Sometimes, I didn't even have a color announcer.

A few years ago, when Jerry Colangelo was still involved, but after the sale of the club, we had a meeting with all our broadcast people before the season. There were probably 30 people in the meeting. Jerry got up and said, "I would just like you all to know, Al and I did all of this by ourselves for years!"

When I started with the Suns, we had a little office on Central Avenue. I was in a little broom closet. I took the brooms out! We had maybe eight people in the entire front office. But we got everything done. That was public relations and radio and TV sales; now we have like 200 employees. There are a lot of other things involved now, like community relations and the suns. com Web site.

In those early years, our training camp was in Lake Havasu City. We trained there for several years in the high school gym. That was an experience, because the locker room was shared by the

Suns and the high school football team. Needless to say, it was a little cramped. From there we went to Prescott, and later Flagstaff, and had some great years training there, too.

In the summer of 1972, the Suns were looking for a head coach. It was a last-minute decision by Jerry Colangelo to hire Willem van Breda Kolff. Some people around the league were surprised, because "Butch" had been around for awhile. He'd coached the Lakers. He'd coached Detroit. But Colangelo was looking for a coach with some experience, so VBK was the guy.

Butch was a character and had a bit of a reputation for how he dealt with people. A little story that depicts the personality of Coach van Breda Kolff comes from Joe Proski. Joe was the trainer of the Suns and always arrived early to get things set for practice. When the team arrived, he told Coach van Breda Kolff that when he had arrived at the high school gym in Lake Havasu, there was a young man who'd been camped out overnight outside. He had hitchhiked from Fresno, California, and said he wanted to try out with the team. When Proski mentioned that to VBK, Butch said, "Hey, give him shoes and workout stuff, and we'll let him play." The next hour, Butch worked that young guy, running him up and down the floor until he almost couldn't move. The guy was close to getting ill. Then, Butch went over to him, reached in his pocket, pulled out a hundred dollar bill, and said, "Buddy, go get a bus ticket. Get back to Fresno and have a good life." Butch did things like that. He just didn't last very long.

It was an interesting year for Butch van Breda Kolff. The very first regular-season game we played, one of the networks came down and wired him, because they wanted to use some of his stuff on future games. The only problem was that 10 minutes into the game, he was ejected.

The Suns had an even 3–3 record when they went to Los Angeles to play the Lakers in the seventh game of the regular season. The Suns starters fell behind in the opening quarter by about 15 points. Coach van Breda Kolff took them all out, and they didn't see another minute of playing time that night. However, the Suns lost the game by only four or five points, and it probably was winnable. After the game, I had an opportunity to ask Butch, "Did you ever think of putting the starters back in?" He used a few words I won't repeat, but said they didn't deserve to play, so they didn't get back in at the end. Then he added, "I'm outta here anyway." The next morning he was. After three wins and four losses in seven games, Butch was relieved of his coaching duties. Jerry Colangelo took over as coach for the first time.

During Butch's tenure, the Suns played preseason games in Puerto Rico—San Juan and Ponce. It was the first time an NBA team had ever played outdoors. In San Juan, the Suns played in an old baseball park, taking on the Milwaukee Bucks. They just put a basketball floor out on the field. The Suns duplicated that experience last year when they played in an outdoor game at the beautiful Indian Wells Tennis Garden in Indian Wells, California. That was only the second time an NBA team had played an outdoor game, and the Suns were involved in both. They did it for a third time during the 2009 preseason.

That trip to San Juan was interesting. I was not doing play-by-play for those games, but I was doing telephone reports. When I got down there that night, they said, "Is anybody broadcasting the game locally?" They said, "Oh, yes. A station here in San Juan is going to be doing the play-by-play." I kept looking for the announcer to show up. I was doing phone-ins, describing the action back to Phoenix. Nobody showed up. As the first quarter ends, I see this young guy running up with all his broadcast equipment. He hooks everything up. I went over to him and said, "Are you doing the play-by-play?" In his broken English, he said, "Yes." I said, "The first quarter has already been played." He said, "Oh, I know, but it's not over yet." So, that was that.

The second game was played in Ponce, and again we played the Bucks. Initially, we were going to bus to Ponce, but they found out it was a rough, mountainous road so they decided to try and get a charter plane to fly us over there. They got this plane, and I had never seen an airplane like it. It only seated about 15 people. There was a roof on it, but where the windows normally were, it was open-air. When the players got on this plane, you can imagine the comments they were making. The pilot was just sitting up front. He wasn't in a protected cockpit. When he got on the plane, he was wearing goggles and a scarf around his neck. The players are making all these comments about him. We flew just over the treetops. Obviously, the pilot had been hearing the comments, because when we finally got to Ponce and landed, he turned around and said in perfect English, "Okay, wise guys. Welcome to Cuba!"

I don't think anybody was surprised at the coaching change. Initially, there were some questions raised when Butch was hired. It was a last-minute move. Jerry Colangelo, who was a stickler for detail, just wasn't pleased with the way training camp and the preseason had gone, and he didn't see that things were going to get better. At that point, he decided he'd coach himself. We were not surprised that Jerry took over the coaching reins. He coached a couple of times in his career.

We had a game in Cleveland in January 1973. The game was played in the old downtown Cleveland Arena. It was a run-down building. The locker rooms had nothing but cold water. Players had to hang their clothes on nails on the walls. The Suns went down to defeat in the worst loss in team history at the time, 111–88. We would finish that season with 38 wins and 44 losses. Butch van Breda Kolff was 3–4, so Colangelo would have been 35 and 40 that year.

After the game, we had to hurry to catch our flight, because we were playing the next night in Detroit. They showed up with a rickety old bus to pick us up at the Cleveland Arena. Halfway to the airport, it just stopped running. They couldn't get it restarted and finally a second bus had to come out to get us. The players were going nuts, because they were freezing in the bus. We got to the airport and just got on the plane as they were getting ready to close the gate.

We get into Detroit, and we're staying at the Hotel Pontchartrain. Jerry Colangelo was pretty low, because the Suns had been embarrassed with that 111–88 loss. We were checking into the hotel a little after midnight, and Jerry said, "Do you feel like a cheeseburger and a beer?" I said, "Why not?" We went out to a place called the Lindell Athletic Club. After we got there, we started talking, and I said, "Jerry, I can't believe you're so easy on these guys. You're the general manager. You're signing their paychecks, and here they embarrass you last night." He got all fired up, too. The next morning, he fines everybody at practice. The next night they lost in Detroit, but by the time the team got to Chicago a couple of days after that, Jerry had cooled down and rescinded the fines. I was concerned, because I was the one who prompted him to fine these guys.

It was great to work with Chick Hearn during the 1975 national broadcast of the NBA **ALL-STAR GAME*** in Phoenix. We'd known each other for a long time, but this was actually the first time we ever got to work together. I don't remember who determined that we would get to work together. It was either Mutual Radio or one of the radio networks the NBA set up for national radio.

Chick was the best-known announcer in the NBA, and the game was in Phoenix, so I was given the nod. Since we knew each other, Chick was amicable about that. He was great to work with. He wanted me to start off the game. He gave me a great introduction, and I still have the cassette tape. Sometimes, when I'm

---

*During the debut of VH1 in 1985, the first image to come on screen was Marvin Gaye singing the national anthem at the NBA **ALL-STAR GAME**.

having a bad day, I get it out and play it, because it makes me think he's introducing someone else. It was very glowing.

I remember that All-Star Game was very competitive. Walt Frazier was named the game's MVP. I still kid Clyde about it. He's on the New York Knicks broadcast team now, and when I see him I say, "Boy, just like 1975, Clyde, when you were in the Coliseum putting them up, right?" The game was sold out. It was the first time we had the All-Star Game here and, of course, it was at the Veterans' Memorial Coliseum.

Twenty years later, in 1995, Phoenix hosted the game again, this time at the America West Arena. The NBA All-Stars came back again in 2009 to the renamed US Airways Center.

It was 1976 when the ABA had their last All-Star Game, and they started a little slam dunk competition. I remember real basketball fans would say, "Hey! Some of the things they do in the ABA aren't that bad." Maybe they didn't go along with the red, white and blue basketball, but they did help change the way they were playing the game. It was an up-tempo game, with a lot of exciting plays. The slam dunk was being used more and that increased interest among fans.

I realized how good the ABA was when I saw Julius Erving. "Dr. J" was such a great player. He really had a lot to do with the eventual merger. Charlie Scott was in the ABA and a lot of other players—Rick Barry, right on down the list. Let's face it. The NBA was starting to realize that the ABA was taking some good players away. Some of the ABA teams wound up in a lot of financial trouble, but some of them did okay, too.

The Suns started off strong in 1975–'76, winning 14 of their first 23 games, but then things were up and down due to injuries. Right around the All-Star break, the Suns made a trade. They sent John Shumate to Buffalo for Garfield Heard, who played for John MacLeod at the University of Oklahoma. At that point in the season, the Suns were struggling, just trying to get back to .500.

They went to New Orleans to play the Jazz on February 20, and that was the night Dick Van Arsdale got hurt. He was undercut on a drive to the basket and broke his wrist. Even though the Suns won that game 103–102, their record was 24–30 on the year. Van went back to Phoenix earlier to have doctors look at the injury, and it looked like he was going to be out for the year. When we left the next morning on the bus, it was a pretty down group of players.

We were on our way to the airport when Coach MacLeod got up, went to the bus driver, and said, "Stop the bus. Pull it off the freeway and park it." Well, the bus driver didn't know what was going on, but did as ordered. I knew that John was not only a good coach but a good friend, and he said what he thought. He pulled that bus over and said, "What are we here for? I know you all are feeling sorry for yourselves, we lost Van, things aren't going well, but what are we all here for?" He went to each individual player and looked right in his eyes. They would say, "We're here to play." "Are you here to compete?" "Yeah, we're here to compete." "If you play, and you compete, you think you can win?"

They finally decided if they did those things, they could win. He said, "Well, let's decide what we're going to do. We played 54 games. We're going to have to play 82 before it's over. Are we going to win them? What are we going to do? Are we going to get in the playoffs?"

Well, that morning they decided they'd make the playoffs. They won 18 of their last 28. They finished 42–40, just over .500, and barely made the playoffs. I've never heard or seen anything like that since. That really picked up the team. Coach MacLeod was able to get into the faces of a few players and get some guys to think about winning. You know, when you lose, it's so easy to think about losing. Now they were going to think about winning. They went out with that attitude every night and got the job done. They surprised the entire NBA world. The Phoenix Suns were in the playoffs.

First up was Seattle, and the Suns beat the Sonics in six games. The Suns were in the Western Conference Finals against the defending NBA champions, the Golden State Warriors, led by Rick Barry. The series went seven games. People forget there was a double overtime game in that series. Keith Erickson, who would become my broadcast partner, had a couple of great games in that series. Game 7 was a classic. It was a Sunday afternoon in Oakland. The game was only a few minutes old when a fan came out of the stands and grabbed the Suns' Curtis Perry. He came out and pushed and grabbed him as if he were going to start a fight. Rick Barry and Ricky Sobers started to mix it up, and Sobers took care of him in a hurry. Boom! Sobers started swinging, and that took the starch out of Rick Barry and the Golden State Warriors. The Suns won that seventh game in Oakland, and I had the opportunity to say something on the radio that I didn't know I would ever get to say: "The Phoenix Suns are going to play for the NBA championship!"

Here's a great story about two great guys: Tom Van Arsdale had retired the year before, but he was with us during those playoffs with his brother Dick. Dick was coming back from a wrist injury and was starting to get some playing time in the playoffs. After the game in Oakland, we had to wait for our plane to make the trip back to Phoenix. John MacLeod had a suite at the hotel, and a lot of the traveling party was hanging out. I just happened to walk into the bedroom of the suite and here were two guys sitting on the bed talking on the telephone. Both of them had tears running down their cheeks. It was Tom and Dick Van Arsdale talking to their mother back in Indiana. Tom was just as happy as if he'd been playing to know his brother was going to be playing in the NBA Finals.

The Suns' opponent was the Boston Celtics. The Boston press was relentless: "Who are these guys in cowboy hats and white socks who think they can stop the Green Machine? It won't be any kind of a Final." The Boston Celtics win the first two games, and it doesn't look too good. We go back to Phoenix, the sellout crowd comes alive, and the Suns win the next two. The Celtics were a little surprised! We go back to Boston for Game 5 on June 4. It was a very hot, humid day, and Boston Garden had no air conditioning. The game did not start until 9 p.m. due to national coverage. You can imagine where all those Boston fans went when they got off at 5 before they came to the Garden.

I showed up to do the game on radio, because it was on national television. My broadcast location at the old Garden was at a higher level. I got up there with my friend Tom Ambrose, who was the Suns' public relations director. He was going to help me with the statistics, because I didn't have a color guy. I noticed they had actually sold the seats next to where I was broadcasting. I said, "Something must be wrong here." Well, about 20 minutes before the game was to start, here come three guys carrying brown bags, and they have the seats right next to me. They're unpacking six packs and wine and having their own party, right there. I asked Tom, "Why don't we get a security guy and get these guys out of here with all this liquor?" Tom goes up to the security guy, who says, "Aw, go pawk your caw. No problem here!" These guys sat there all during the game, and everytime Boston did something good, I got it on the arm.

The Suns got off to a horrible start, and it looks like they were going to be blown out. But they kept battling back and, before you knew it, we're getting down to the last few minutes, and the game was tied. Now we go to overtime and battle again. The players are beaten up. It's so hot and humid in that building. No one can pull it out, so we go to the second overtime. Then we had the famous "shot heard around the world" by Gar Heard that sent it into the amazing third overtime.

The big discrepancy in that game was when Paul Silas, former Sun and then a Boston Celtic, tried to call a timeout after Boston had used all of theirs. The rule has since been changed, but at that time, when you had used all you allotted timeouts and tried to call another one, it was a technical foul. Richie Powers was one of the two refs working the game. Paul Silas was right in his face trying to call the timeout. The Suns should have had their free throw and could have won the game. Richie Powers did not make that call. Later, he said that he was not going to let a championship be decided by that type of call. I didn't know he was there to make that kind of decision. I guess he thought he was there to make the rules. The game was eventually won, 128–126, by the Celtics. But the Suns had arrived.

One of the stories I've told many times about that amazing Game 5 centers around the moment when Gar Heard hits that shot, and the Boston fan sitting next to me jumped up and passed out on my lap. I'm trying to get him off my lap to see what's going on. The fans had just gone out on the floor, because they thought the game was over, that the shot didn't count, and Boston had won. Of course, it did count. I pushed the guy off my lap.

After the game was over, we were all in the locker room, and Jerry Colangelo walked in. He said, "We're walking out of here with our heads up. If anyone says anything to you, you can do what you want." We had to walk right by the Boston locker room. As we walked out, Red Auerbach was standing there. Jerry stopped, looked at him, and said, "No security. I'm tired of this place." Red said, "Nothing wrong, Jerry. Nothing wrong."

During that whole game, especially in the fourth quarter, our players were constantly being threatened by the surrounding fans. Some were even trying to punch our players. There was no security. It was unbelievable. We were up high during the broadcast and then went down with the team to walk out. I wouldn't have walked out alone. During the fourth quarter, MacLeod could hardly talk to his team during a timeout. He had to pull the whole team out to center court to communicate. There was talk right away that Game 5 could have been the best NBA game ever.

After that triple overtime game, we went back to the hotel to Jerry Colangelo's suite. John MacLeod was there, along with assistant coach Al Bianchi. We can't get over the fact that Richie Powers didn't make the call at that crucial point in the game. By now it's about 2:30 in the morning, and there is a knock on the door. In walks Mendy Rudolph and Rick Barry, who had been the commentators on the national CBS telecast. They were not even staying in our hotel, but they had been talking about the game and said they just had to come over. They could not believe Powers didn't make the call and how it turned out. We stayed up all night. At six o'clock that morning, we went downstairs to get some coffee and breakfast. Then we headed back to Phoenix.

Following that series, Phoenix sports columnist Joe Gilmartin did a book called *The Little Team That Could and Darn Near Did!* It was an amazing team. There were no huge superstars, just a great bunch of guys who wanted to win. We talked about Alvan Adams and Ricky Sobers. Sobers was a very tough, competitive guy. When Van Arsdale was out, Ricky really stepped up. Dennis Awtrey played that whole series with a broken foot. He was the backup center behind Alvan Adams. Game 5 was a tough loss, but it really turned Phoenix into an NBA city.

That summer, I was back in Williams, Iowa, for the Fourth of July celebration—a big deal there. They have a parade during the day and a big celebration in the park. The American Legion was putting it on, and they had a flatbed truck there with a **P.A. SYSTEM***. The commander asked if I would get up and talk about the triple overtime game. He told me, "Everyone would love to hear about it." I got up and talked about it a little bit. I told them a writer I knew from New York came up to me and said, "Al, you know a lot of people already are saying this is the greatest basketball game ever played. How would you rank it?" I said, "Obviously they have never seen Williams play Blairsburg!" Blairsburg was our big rival in Williams. That got big applause.

The next year there were high expectations, but also injuries to Gar Heard, Curtis Perry, and Alvan Adams. We were healthy

---

*The **PUBLIC ADDRESS ANNOUNCER** for the Houston Colt '45s (later the Astros) in their 1962 inaugural season was Dan Rather...the P.A. announcer for the Brooklyn Dodgers in 1936 and 1937 was John Forsythe, later a TV and movie star.

with all of our starters for only six games the entire season. But that year Connie Hawkins was put in the Suns Ring of Honor and No. 42 was hung in the Coliseum rafters. He was such a factor in putting the Suns franchise on the map. We went to the playoffs against the Lakers right after he got here. He was a great player and one of the most creative. Julius Erving will tell you that everything he did he learned from watching Hawk. When I joined the Suns, Hawk was at the tail end of his career. He was still amazing.

My great Hawk story comes right after Hawk's book *Foul!* came out. The book was written by David Wolf. We were on a long road trip, and every place we went, they wanted Hawk to do some interviews to promote the book. We were in Chicago and would finish the road trip in Omaha. The **KANSAS CITY*** Kings were playing some games in Omaha at that time. David Wolf had joined us to work with Hawk to make sure he was doing these interviews. We lost a tough overtime game in Chicago and were on a morning flight the next day to Omaha. Remember, we always had to take the first flight out in those days. Hawk is sitting with me on the plane. He said, "David Wolf is going to be over there, and I'm supposed to do an interview at the airport. Man, I'm so tired and beat after that game. I don't know. I don't know."

We get to the airport in Omaha, and David Wolf isn't there. He had taken a later flight, but the two guys from the newspaper were there for the interview. Hawk stayed with them, and we went to the hotel. Later, it's close to game time. I'm down in the locker room before the game and no Hawk. I say to Prosk, "Hey! Where's Hawk?" Prosk says, "I don't know. I've been trying to call his room. I don't know where he is. No one answers the phone." I walk out to my broadcast position without knowing what's going on. I look up and see David Wolf walk into the arena. He looks around, and all of a sudden he takes off.

*The Oakland A's colors are green and gold because their late owner, Charles O. Finley, grew up in La Porte, Indiana and loved Notre Dame... when he bought the **KANSAS CITY** *A's, he changed their uniforms to the Notre Dame colors...The Green Bay Packers also adopted Notre Dame colors because Curly Lambeau played at Notre Dame.*

It turns out that after all these interviews were done, David Wolf showed up on a later flight. He and Hawk have a late lunch, go back to the hotel, and David says, "Just lie down in my room here. I'm going to be out doing some stuff, but I'll be back." Well, he didn't come back, and here's Hawk sound asleep in Wolf's room, and no one can get hold of him. Wolf, when he gets to the arena, sees Hawk isn't there and knows what happened. He races back to the hotel to get Hawk, who arrives about 15 minutes before game time.

We still didn't know what had happened. He comes down without his shoes, so we have to send a **BALLBOY*** back to get them. Now it's the end of the first quarter. I'm doing the game near the aisle that goes back into the locker room. I turn around and there's Hawk, standing there. It's the end of the first quarter. I turn around and looked at Hawk, "Hawk! What's going on, man? Where have you been?" He looked at me and said, "Well Al, look at it this way, if this were baseball and we were playing a doubleheader, I'd be early for the second game." That was Hawk. He was the greatest.

As I said, the 1976–'77 season brought a lot of expectations, but also a lot of injuries. The next year, we have a first-round draft pick, and we pick a guy named Walter Davis from North Carolina. He was the fifth player picked in the first round, so our bad year turned out good. Walter Davis was one of the greatest shooters ever to play this game. I called him "The Man with the Velvet Touch." He had a great career at **NORTH CAROLINA***. Coach Dean Smith was very high on Walter.

*Jon Gruden, in 2003 became the youngest coach to win a Super Bowl, was a quarterback at Muskingum before transferring to the University of Dayton...Gruden was a **BALLBOY** for the undefeated 1976 Indiana basketball team.

*Michael Jordan was given his first set of golf clubs by fellow University of **NORTH CAROLINA** classmate Davis Love, Davis Love, Davis Love.... In 1994, the White Sox recalled Michael Jordan from Double-A Birmingham to play against the Cubs in the Mayor's Trophy Game at Wrigley Field. Jordan singled and doubled against the Cubs.

When Walter came into the NBA, even in practice before the pre-season, you could just see what a fluid player he was. He could run the floor, had a great shot, and was just a terrific guy. He became the NBA Rookie of the Year that season. The Suns won 49 games and set record attendance figures. After that bad year, Walter Davis made a tremendous impact. He was, as I said, one of the best pure shooters ever to wear a Suns uniform. He used to tell me that when he was seven or eight years old, he would think nothing of going out all day and shooting 350–400 shots—every day, seven days a week. Great players aren't necessarily born, they work at it, and Walter did. He won a lot of games in a Suns uniform.

The next year, the Suns did great. They won 50 games and made a nice trade to get Truck Robinson in midseason. He proved to be a great rebounder and defender and helped the Suns get into the playoffs. That might have been one of the years that the Suns should have won the championship. They went into the playoffs and beat Portland and Kansas City. But in the Western Conference Finals, they lost to Seattle in seven games. They held a 3–2 edge in that series, but couldn't hang on.

The next year, '79–'80, they won 55 games. Dennis Johnson was named to the NBA's first-team All-Defensive Team that year. DJ was a great defender and player and a likable guy. It's hard to believe he lost his life at such an early age.

I guess the biggest thing for the Suns that year was the arrival of the Gorilla on the scene. Everyone wants to know how the Gorilla evolved. During that season, somebody at the Coliseum had hired a singing telegram company, Eastern Onion, to sing Happy Birthday to someone at the game. The guy delivering the message happened to show up wearing a gorilla suit. The fans had so much fun with him that some of our Suns' marketing people, Harvey Shank and some of his crew, said, "Hey! We better find out who that was!" As the Gorilla was leaving that day, the ball bounced over to him, and he did something with it before giving it to the ref. The fans really responded to that. The team thought the Gorilla might be a clever way to create fan interest, and a star was born. The Gorilla was one of the first basketball mascots.

The San Diego Chicken was probably the first mascot to really make a name for himself in sports, but I don't think our Gorilla has to take a backseat to him or any other mascot. It's amazing how many mascots around the NBA are former ASU gymnasts. There are at least a half a dozen of them.

In 1983, Larry Nance won the NBA's first slam dunk contest as a rookie. He was a great player, but really evolved when he was traded to Cleveland. He became a great player for them.

That year, something happened to me that has happened only once in my career. The Suns were on their way to a game in Denver and had flown in that morning. We were at the airport waiting for our luggage. It seemed like it was taking a long time, and I started looking for a bathroom. Well, I found the bathroom, but when I came out, the luggage and the bus were gone. Coach John MacLeod decided to leave me at the airport. He knew I was missing. I had to take a cab. That was the only time I missed a bus, and we used to have a lot of early bus rides.

Coach MacLeod was one of those guys who insisted his eight o'clock bus leave at 7:55. He was notorious for leaving people. As a matter of fact, the great Walter Davis didn't get any breaks either. The Suns were in Milan, Italy, and we were going to play a game about 30 miles away. It was about 3:50, and Walter Davis wasn't on the four o'clock bus yet. Coach MacLeod asked trainer Joe Proski, "Where's Walter?" Joe said, "I just checked. He's on his way down." Five minutes later, Walter wasn't down, so we left. Walter had to take a **CAB***.

*During one off-season, Celtics center Dave Cowens drove a **CAB** in Boston. He claimed he took only one passenger the "long way" because the passenger was an obnoxious Knicks fan.

The night Paul Westphal had his career high in Detroit, we had another early morning flight, with the same result. We had an 8 a.m. bus. It was 10 minutes til, and Paul wasn't there. Proski went inside to check and said he wasn't answering and must be on his way. Five minutes later, we left. Coach MacLeod's been known to leave a few guys. We left Curtis Perry in New Orleans one morning. The bus pulled away, and here comes Curtis running with his two suitcases, unable to catch up. Coaches used to be a little tougher. That's changed.

In 1985, we had a Suns reunion. Jerry Colangelo wanted to bring back a lot of the former players. Twenty-four former Suns showed up and even played an exhibition game before one of the Suns' regular season games. Players like Clem Haskins, the Van Arsdales, Curtis Perry, and Gar Heard all came out. That's when Neal Walk first encountered some of the problems that would ultimately cause him to be paralyzed from the waist down. He had come out to the Suns reunion from New York and was playing Frisbee the night before the game. He thought he hurt his back, so he wound up not playing in the game. Eventually, a tumor was discovered.

Neal had some great years with the Suns and was always one of my favorite guys. When the Suns lost the coin flip to Milwaukee, Phoenix took Neal. Milwaukee selected Lew Alcindor, a.k.a. Kareem Abdul-Jabbar. He had some great years and still holds rebounding records for the Suns. In his best year, he averaged more than 20 points, more than 12 **REBOUNDS***, and was one of the better true centers that the Suns had ever had. When the Suns had that reunion in 1985, Neal was working for a small advertising agency in New York and had not been back to Phoenix in quite awhile. He came back that weekend and had a great time. He saw a lot of his old friends and former teammates.

*The one fundamental that transfers to pro basketball from college basketball is great **REBOUNDING**.

But after playing Frisbee and hurting his back, he elected to sit out the reunion game. After doctors put Neal through various tests and some surgeries, they thought he had something wrong with his shoulder and neck. They finally found a tumor wrapped around his spinal cord, but didn't know whether it was malignant or not. To remove it, there is always the possibility that the surgery could cause paralysis. The decision was made to go for the surgery. The growth was not malignant, but the surgery left him paralyzed from the waist down. Neal is now in a wheelchair and still works for the Suns in our Archiving Department. He's just as tough a competitor today as he was as a player. In 1990, he received the "Wheelchair Athlete of the Year" award at the White House from President George Bush.

At one time in their careers, Neal Walk and Connie Hawkins played together in Italy and were very close. After Neal was in a wheelchair, the two had not seen each other in a number of years. Hawk walked into the Suns office and saw Neal in his wheelchair and just broke down.

After missing the playoffs in 1986 for the first time in nine years, the Suns went into the '86–'87 season not quite up to par. John MacLeod was in his 14th year as the head coach, but the Suns weren't playing well, and Jerry Colangelo was concerned. We were leaving one morning to play the Lakers. I was in the office and sensed something was going on. I went to see Jerry and said, "Jerry, are you going to make a coaching change?" He looked at me and said, "Yeah, I'm going to make you the coach!" I told him that if he didn't want to say anything, it was okay.

Now we're in L.A. playing the Lakers, and the game is on radio and television. Dick Van Arsdale was my analyst. John MacLeod always came out before the game to tape a TV interview with me. I'm waiting down on the floor. Dick Van Arsdale walked over to me and said, "You know what's going on, don't you? John's going to be fired after the game tonight." I said, "What are they going to do?" Van said, "I'm going to take over." Well, here comes John, and the conversation stops. Dick leaves, and I do the interview with Coach MacLeod. I know, but he doesn't. Finally, we get up to the broadcast location. We're doing a lot of stuff, and I don't get the chance to really get into anything with Dick. During a timeout I say, "Dick, what are you doing?" He said, "Well, after the game, they're going to let John go, and I'm going to take over." I told him, "You haven't even been to a practice all year. How are you going to coach this team? How about John Wetzel?" "They're going to let him go, too," he told me. "We have to talk about this. What are you doing after the game?" He said, "Well, I have some people here from Indiana." I said, "Joe Proski and I will be in the bar. Whenever you get back, come in."

After the game was over, we go back to the hotel, and I proceed to tell Proski what's going on. He says, "What's Van going to do? He hasn't been to a practice all year. They have to keep Wetzel." Pretty soon, here comes Dick Van Arsdale back from having something to eat with his friends. We grab him and say, "You've got to keep Wetz. He's the only one who knows the plays and what's going on." Dick starts to think about it and says, "Well, I guess I better get back to Phoenix before you guys so I can talk to Jerry and tell him I want Wetz to stay."

Joe gets on the phone and gets an early flight out for Dick so he can get back to Phoenix before the team does. The next morning we didn't have a team bus, but had hotel transportation take us to the airport. Who happens to be on the van? John MacLeod, John Wetzel, me and Joe Proski. Should you say anything? Should you ask anything? I decide that it's not going to do me any good to say anything. In a few minutes, MacLeod turns around and says, "Well, I'm not going to be seeing you guys much anymore."

"What do you mean?" we ask. "Well, I had a message from Jerry that he wants to see me as soon as we get in. I don't think I'm going to get an extension."

The Suns were 22–34 at the time Dick Van Arsdale took over. He calls himself a winning coach because the Suns went 14–12 the rest of the way under Van. After that, he decided he never wanted to coach again.

The next year, John Wetzel was named the head coach, and Cotton Fitzsimmons came back to the team as director of player personnel. In late February, a trade was made that a lot of people questioned at the time. Larry Nance was traded to Cleveland for Kevin Johnson, Mark West, and a draft pick that eventually became Dan Majerle. At the end of that season, guess who was back and named the head coach? Cotton Fitzsimmons. In his first year back, we went from winning 28 games to winning 55. At the time, that was the third biggest turnaround in NBA history. Cotton was the best. I miss him every day. The Suns set an attendance record that year, and the awards piled up. Eddie Johnson won the Sixth Man of the Year Award, Kevin Johnson was named Most Improved Player, Cotton Fitzsimmons was named Coach of the Year, and Jerry Colangelo was named Executive of the Year. The Suns got to the Western Conference Finals, but that was all. The next year also ended with a trip to the Western Conference Finals.

The last season the Suns played at the Coliseum was 1991–'92. The game that I remember best was the last game ever played at the Coliseum. It was a playoff game against Portland on May 11. Kevin Johnson scored 35 points, and the game went to double overtime, but Portland won, 153–151. The next game, at Portland, the Suns were bounced from the playoffs. It had been a tough series and year, but as they walked off the floor in Portland, assistant coach Lionel Hollins said, "What this team needs is a Charles Barkley." If only he knew that was going to happen.

Although the next year proved to be an unbelievable season, any time you make a controversial trade, emotions can run high. Jeff Hornacek was a favorite in Suns country, but you're going to have to give something up to get something, and Charles Barkley was the type of player the Suns needed. They needed a rebounder. They needed a defender. They needed an aggressive player, and that's what Charles was.

The 1992–'93 season is one that Suns fans will always remember. We moved into a new building, got a new coach in Paul Westphal, picked up a new star player in Charles Barkley, and even got new uniforms that year.

Nobody expected the success of the 1976 season. But in '92–'93, it was expected, and the Suns didn't disappoint. They won 62 games—the best record in the NBA—and the Pacific Division title. In the month of December, they won all 14 games, and Paul was on his way to becoming the winningest first-year coach in NBA history. It was a great team—Dan Majerle, Charles, just an unbelievable team. Charles was the first Sun to be named as the NBA's MVP. The club also led the league in scoring. Led by "Thunder Dan" Majerle, the team set a record for three-point shots made. With the new building and a winning team, the Suns set an attendance record. But, oh my, the playoffs were even more exciting.

You could tell by the way they played that this team was capable of great things. That was Charles' greatest year. He really wanted to win and was just such a competitive guy. He had the excitement and enthusiasm and wasn't going to let this team lose. He was the fan favorite and was more popular than you can imagine.

The fact that he was such an aggressive, competitive player made him so wonderful that year. When you talk about rebounding, I've heard a lot of players, including Charles, say, "It's not the biggest guy who gets the rebound. It's the guy who wants it most!" Charles wanted it the most. He was only about 6'5" or 6'6", but he could get the ball away from a guy who was 6'10". He could score. He could pass. His attitude was that he would just not let that team lose and, 62 times that year, they didn't.

That year, the opening playoff series was a best of five. The Suns took on the hated Lakers in the first round and promptly lost the first two games. The fans were down. Everyone was down. But Paul Westphal says without hesitation, "We will win three straight. Don't worry about it!." He said that to the media, the fans, everybody. I liked his attitude. The Suns won three straight, the last one in overtime, and they eliminated the Lakers. The locker room was crazy.

Then the Suns took San Antonio in six games. Yes, they have beaten San Antonio—people forget about that. After that series, they eliminated Seattle in seven games. It was on to Chicago and a showdown between Charles and Michael Jordan.

There was a triple overtime game in that series. The Suns won that game 129-121 in the old Chicago Stadium. So the Suns did win a triple overtime game in the NBA Finals after losing to Boston in 1976. Many people feel that Michael Jordan was the biggest factor in Chicago's eventual championship. He played well in the series, but the guy who broke the Suns' back was a fellow named John Paxson, who hit the deciding three-pointer in Game 6 to defeat the Suns and give the championship to the Chicago Bulls.

Danny Ainge says he still wakes up in the middle of the night wondering why he didn't jump out and defend Paxson. The Suns defense thought the Bulls were going to go inside for the last shot, so they sagged down defensively. That left John Paxson wide open at the three-point line. They went inside first but then threw it back out to a wide-open Paxson. Ainge tried to hustle back but couldn't get to Paxson in time. Paxson's three-pointer swished through the net, and the Suns' hopes for a championship were crushed.

More recently, John has been in the front office of the Chicago Bulls. He is a great guy, but every time I see him I say, "Don't talk to me. I don't want to hear about it, John." He'll always be the guy who hit the big shot. Our team, which was one of the best groups to ever put on Suns uniforms, still feels they should have won that series with Chicago—but it's another "what if?" situation.

Barkley had some great games for the Suns. He hit a big shot over David Robinson to win the San Antonio series. I thought the '92-'93 season was the best season Charles Barkley ever had in the NBA. He adopted an attitude where he would not let the Suns lose. They only lost 20 times that year. He was miraculous with his intensity. He was a great rebounder and defender, and he hit the key shot when you needed it most. It was a Suns team that really had the type of aggressiveness needed to win a championship. But thanks to John Paxson of Chicago, it didn't happen. But that season Charles was Charles! He was always giving the writers and broadcasters plenty to talk about.

The next year, '93–'94, the Suns won 56 games, ending the season with seven straight wins. In one of those last games against San Antonio, Kevin Johnson had an amazing 25 assists. The Suns had a lot of injuries that year but still had a strong season. In the playoffs, they beat Golden State. Again, Charles Barkley had one of his great games in Game 3 of that series against the Warriors, scoring 56 points. He just wouldn't let his team lose.

The Suns then ran into the Houston Rockets, which was to happen two years in a row. They lost to Houston in a hard-fought seven-game series that decided the West, and Houston went on to win the championship.

The very next season, 1994–'95, the Suns won 59 games and the Pacific Division, then got into the playoffs and beat Portland. But...here comes Houston again. In that series, the Suns had a 3-1 lead over Houston, but the Rockets, in overtime, won Game 7 by one point—and once again went on to win the NBA title. That was tough.

The 45th NBA All-Star Game was in Phoenix again in 1995. Paul Westphal was the coach, and Charles Barkley and Dan Majerle of the Suns were both on the Western Conference team.

Following that 1995 season, there were coaching changes. Cotton Fitzsimmons took over for Westphal on a temporary basis and then Danny Ainge assumed the role of head coach. The Suns had a pretty good year; however, not a championship-caliber year. Rex Chapman, the former Kentucky All-American, was with the Suns that season, and there were games when he really put on a show. One night against Seattle, he scored 41 points and hit nine three-pointers in the process. Shazam! But the Suns lost the game.

The next year, the Suns got off to a good start—they were 13-7— but Danny Ainge decided that coaching wasn't quite as much fun as he thought it was going to be. Danny stepped down and assistant coach Scott Skiles took over. Skiles coached the Suns for one full season and a major portion of two others before Frank Johnson took over the coaching reins in February 2001. In 2003 Mike D'Antoni, an understudy as an assistant coach, steps up to start his era with the Suns.

In 2004, the Suns have a new owner, Robert Sarver. Robert grew up in Tucson and attended the University of Arizona. When the rumors first started flying that the Suns were being sold, Jerry Colangelo decided that they better have a press conference before all the rumors beat them to the announcement. He picked up Sarver, who came in from Tucson, and was showing him around the coaches' offices at what was now US Airways Center. When they came to my office, Robert looked in and said, "You don't have to introduce me to this guy. I've been listening to him since I was 10 years old." Robert has been terrific as the owner.

That year, 2004–'05, the Suns again had a big season. They won 62 games, equaling their previous best in 1992–'93. The Suns' road record was an amazing 31–10. That was the team that featured Steve Nash, Amaré Stoudemire, Shawn Marion, and Joe Johnson. "JJ" led the way—he was tops in scoring—and had more three-pointers than anyone in the league that season. Unfortunately, in the first round of the playoffs against Memphis, Joe was injured and unavailable for any remaining playoff games.

The Suns started a series of seasons where they played great basketball and were right on the edge of winning a championship, but something always happened. The first thing was that year when Joe Johnson was injured. The Suns managed to defeat Dallas in six, but their old bugaboo—the San Antonio Spurs—came back to beat them in the Western Conference Finals. San Antonio then went on to win the NBA title. For the next few years, the Suns enjoyed their winning ways with 54-, 61-, and 55-win seasons, but San Antonio always seemed to be in the way.

There were some tense moments against San Antonio. Probably one that is still hard to accept was the game in San Antonio when

Robert Horry completely low-bridged the Suns' Steve Nash, trying to physically hurt him and take him out of the game. It happened right in front of our broadcast location. I thought my color guy, Tim Kempton, was going to jump up and punch Horry out because it was the most vicious hit I ever recall seeing in an NBA game. Horry just ran at Nash and hit him with a hockey-style check, knocking him right into the press table.

When that happened, the Suns' Boris Diaw and Amaré Stoudemire stepped up, away from the bench, to look down and see what had happened to Nash. As a result of that, our league decided to suspend them for the next game. Again, it was one of those things that happened against San Antonio. Although the Suns battled hard, they were without two of their key players— and they lost. That will forever be one of the more controversial things ever to happen in the NBA playoffs.

Ironically, earlier in that Game 2 San Antonio players had come out on the floor from their bench, but the league decided to do nothing to them. It was a tough situation. In those few years with Mike D'Antoni, when the Suns were winning and had great games, it seemed like there was always a problem that popped up to prevent them from getting to the championship round.

Finally the D'Antoni era was over, and Steve Kerr, the former U of A and NBA performer who had come in as general manager the year before, took over. His first hire was Terry Porter, a former player. Porter had been an assistant coach and briefly a head coach in the NBA, and he took over when D'Antoni left, under not the best terms. There were some disagreements on the direction of the club from the front office. Mike left and wound up signing a very lucrative contract with the New York Knicks.

But the coaching change with Terry Porter was not successful. By the All-Star Game in February, Terry was relieved of his coaching duties. Alvin Gentry, a longtime assistant with the Suns and head coach in the NBA, took over the coaching reins, and he remains the head coach today.

The Suns had their 2009 training camp at the University of San Diego. The arena there is named after, and donated by, Jenny Craig, who is one of the owners of the Suns. Her husband just passed away this past year. She is a wonderful person. You will never meet a nicer, down-to-earth lady than Jenny Craig. She had this arena built on the University of San Diego campus, so that's where the Suns trained this year.

Maybe the most interesting place the Suns trained was in Italy when Mike D'Antoni was coaching the team. We trained in Italy and played preseason games in Rome and Cologne, Germany, that year. It was great training in Italy, because Mike D'Antoni had played and coached there for many years and was greeted like an idol. He was so loved there that every place we went, he and his wife were mobbed. We had a full house at a game there with one of the Italian teams. I believe he still has a dual citizenship.

When we trained in Italy, I broadcast the Rome and Cologne games on radio back to Phoenix. When we were in Rome, I was standing down on the floor, and I was very surprised, because people started coming to me and asking me for my autograph. Finally, after about the fourth or fifth person, there was a lady who came up and called me by name. I said, "Why do you want my autograph?" She said, "We hear all your games on the Internet." It was the same in Cologne. They all heard the Suns games on the Internet. They came up and called me by name. One fellow even said, "Please write *Shazam!* on my program." Whether the league realizes it or not, one of the most important marketing tools they have is the NBA team radio broadcasts, which go worldwide on the Internet.

In 1990, we opened the regular season in Tokyo, Japan, playing the first two games against the Utah Jazz. Our last preseason game was in Chicago. Coach Cotton Fitzsimmons was trying to figure out how to get the team ready to adjust to the new time zone. He decided to keep everybody up all night, have the team sleep on the plane, and wake up in Tokyo. There was a little Italian restaurant we loved in Chicago, and the owner decided he'd stay up 'til four or five o'clock in the morning with us. But it just didn't work. The players got to Tokyo and wanted to sleep then. We played the first two games on November 2 and 3, 1990, in Tokyo, before more than 10,000 people. We won the first game against the Jazz and then lost the second. It was the first time that professional sports teams from the United States had played regular-season games outside of North America.

Tokyo was something else—just the fast train in from the airport would knock your socks off. And the congestion and traffic. I did one experiment while I was in Tokyo. Hot Rod Hundley, who was the voice of the Utah Jazz, and I did the simulcast—radio and TV—together. The same broadcast went to Utah and Arizona. We were filming some stuff for our pregame show one day and, as an experiment, I was going to set my briefcase across the street on the sidewalk and see what would happen—if anyone would take it. I didn't trust anybody, so I took everything of value out of it. I took my big leather briefcase to the other side of the street, laid it right in the middle of the sidewalk, and left it there for the hour we were filming. Not only was it still there, but no one had even touched it. The amount of foot traffic was unbelievable. In any city in America, that briefcase would have been gone in about 30 seconds.

The Japanese crowds really knew what was going on. There are so many sports publications in Japan and Europe, and the fans know a lot about the players. They would call them out by name. Tokyo was a little different, because sometimes they whistle rather than applaud, but they were very enthusiastic about the game. The players were excited about going over there to play, because not that many players had been there. Now, it's a little different, because NBA players have been all over the world. Setting aside the historical significance of the trip, we came back a little worried that the jet lag might affect the team for awhile, but we came back to the States and won the next three.

When New Jersey first came into the league, they didn't have their own gym. They were playing their games at various college gyms or wherever they could hang their hat for a while. Originally, they played at Rutgers University. One time, our bus driver got lost going to the game. We got in there late at night, and I get up to my room, take the bags in, and look around. There's no bed. There's a couch...there's a desk...but there's no bed. I call downstairs, and the guy on the desk was a little confused. I said, "I'm in this room, and there's no bed." He said, "Oh, there has to be." I said, "There is no bed. I need another room." He said, "We don't have any other rooms. We're sold out."

Finally, I go down to the front desk and try to get another room, but they were sold out. He finally figures out what the problem was. The room they had given me was part of a suite, but someone was in the other part. Here I am in the part of the suite that has no bed. Fortunately, after about half an hour, they were able to find a rollaway someplace for me. I'd have to say that was probably my worst night.

The runner-up was in Portland, Oregon, where we used to stay in a hotel right by the Coliseum. It was also right by the train tracks. Even our players complained about this. My room happened to be on the edge closest to the railroad tracks. All night long, you heard the trains going by.

There was a similar situation in Atlanta. We got in late, but had the next day off. I had about a $10 cab ride to get from the lobby to my room—it was a long way off. I had all my bags, and there was no bellman on duty. I walk into the room, and it's a complete mess. There'd been a big party in the room, and there was broken glass—it was horrible. I call the front desk, and it's just like New Jersey. I told him, "This room has not been made up." He said, "Just a moment, sir." He comes back on the phone, "Oh yes, that room has been made up." I said, "The room has not been made up." "Well, I just checked the computer, and it has been made up." I said, "I'm in the room. The room has not been made up. I need another room." Since the computer says the room has been made up, this guy does not believe it. I asked him, "Would you please send somebody up to the room? I don't care who. You come up or send anybody else. I'm in the room. It's a total mess. **WORLD WAR III*** has taken place here, and it has not been made up." Finally, someone came up, and I ended up getting another room. They would not believe me because the computer said the room had been made up.

We're in Boston playing the Celtics and, as you may know, a lot of people get hotel rooms to have parties. As I was getting ready to leave for the game in the late afternoon, I saw a few young guys checking into the room right next door to me. I noticed they were bringing in a lot of various libations, which made me a little nervous.

After the game, I get back to the hotel. We have an early departure the next morning, because in those days, when you were flying commercial, it was required by the NBA that you had to take the first flight out the following morning after a game, so we were leaving the hotel about six o'clock in the morning. I get into bed about midnight. I hadn't been in bed more than 10 or 15 minutes when the party started rocking next door. I mean it was unbelievable. These guys went at it until four o'clock in the morning. I called down to the front desk to complain, but nothing was done. I was awake from midnight until 4 a.m. and had to get up at 5 a.m. Starting at five o'clock, I called their room every five minutes. I could hear them. They'd get up and answer the phone, and I'd hang up. I let five more minutes go by, and I'd call again. They'd get up, and I'd hang up. This went on for half an hour. They were yelling and screaming and practically throwing things at the phone, but I got my due!

In the NBA today, we stay only at premier hotels. It would be difficult to pinpoint the best—the hotel in Beverly Hills is very good.

---

*The first American to jump off the boats at the **D-DAY** invasion was James Arness of "Gunsmoke" fame. At 6' 7", he was the tallest man on the first ship and the ship's captain wanted to test how deep the water was.

We stay at a lot of Four Seasons and Ritz Carltons, which are great, so we're spoiled. It's a little bit different from the early days.

The rigors of traveling with a pro sports team require you to watch your diet. Through the years, I have found what works best for me—vitamin supplements and watching my diet. So far, it's worked pretty well. In those Iowa days, it was meat and potatoes, believe me. I still like the pork tenderloins and the Maid-Rites. When I get back to Iowa, I can't turn those down.

When you're doing a lot of traveling, and you get a night off in places like New York, Chicago or L.A., you really want to enjoy it, and you begin to learn where the better restaurants are. Being a guy from Iowa, on a lot of nights the popcorn keeps me going. Now, with our charter plane, we leave after games, and the food on the plane is probably not that conducive to great health. That's when I lean back and say, "Well, I'll just have some popcorn tonight."

Hot Rod Hundley was my first color announcer. He had just come from working with Chick Hearn, the Lakers' longtime announcer and one of the all-time greats. Hot Rod was terrific. He gave me a good indoctrination to the NBA, both on and off the court. In 1972, the NBA played ABA teams for the first time, in exhibition games. We were down in Louisville, Kentucky. There were four teams there—Philadelphia and Phoenix of the NBA and Indiana and Kentucky from the ABA. I had a little background with the ABA, because the very first broadcast I did in September of 1972 was Phoenix at Salt Lake City against the ABA's Utah Stars, who were coached by basketball legend **BILL SHARMAN***. Years later, when I got the Curt Gowdy Award from

*__BILL SHARMAN__ was once kicked out of a major league baseball game even though he never played in one. An outstanding outfielder in the "loaded" Brooklyn Dodgers farm system, he was called up to the major league club in September, 1951. During a Dodger game at Wrigley Field home plate umpire Jocko Conlan, tired of heckling from the Dodger dugout, ejected every player sitting in the dugout including Sharman.

the Basketball Hall of Fame, the guy across the hall in my hotel was Bill Sharman. We had a nice talk about that first game when he was coaching the Utah Stars.

I remember the Suns playing Indiana in this exhibition game in Louisville, Kentucky. Hot Rod was my color announcer. Indiana had a big forward—I think it was George McGinnis—who had a nice little 15-foot turnaround jump shot. That was one of the keys to his offensive game. At some point, Big George hits this shot. I turned to Hot Rod and said, "That's really been his bread and butter. That little turnaround 15-foot jumper is really his best shot. Rod, you were an All-American in college, an NBA player. What was your favorite shot?" He said, "Cutty and water," and we went right on like nothing had ever happened. That's the kind of thing Hot Rod could do. The "Cutty" was Cutty Sark Scotch, of course!

Hot Rod knew I was a piano player, so he always looked for a piano bar when we were on the road with a night off. There used to be a little bar with a piano in Kansas City just a little ways from the Muehlebach Hotel where a lot of players and coaches used to go. If we had a night off in Kansas City, Hot Rod would be there, and he'd put an empty glass on the piano. He'd get me to sit down and play, and then he'd take all the tips. It usually took care of his bar bill. Hot Rod was one of my favorite color announcers, no question about it...and a great guy.

When the city of Phoenix got its NBA franchise, it was called just that, "NBA franchise." No name. Jerry Colangelo got with *The Arizona Republic* and came up with a contest to name the team. I can tell you there were some lousy entries. Some that I'm glad didn't make it. The "Prickly Pears" was one I remember. Could you imagine saying that? "The Sheriffs," the "Mustangs" and the "Rattlesnakes" were just some of the names submitted. "Suns" was the first choice, of course, but there were a number of entries suggesting "Suns," so they had a drawing, and Mrs. Selinda King was the winner. As I recall, she got season tickets for that year, and the Suns got their name.

CHIEF ILLINI

Jerry Colangelo

Jerry Colangelo started his sports management career in 1966 doing marketing and scouting for the Chicago Bulls. Two years later he was named general manager of the expansion Phoenix franchise. At 28 years of age, he was the youngest general manager in professional sports. In his 40 year tenure with the Phoenix franchise, he served as coach (a 59-60 career record), president, managing general partner, CEO and chairman. For many years he served as chairman of the NBA's board of governors. Currently, he is chairman of the board for the gold medal winning USA Men's Basketball program. A member of the Suns Ring of Honor, he was inducted into the Basketball Hall of Fame in 2004.

It's hard to remember the first time I laid eyes on Al McCoy, because when I got to Phoenix in 1968, I heard Al's voice everywhere. He was doing minor league baseball and hockey. He was also on one of the local radio stations doing sports. I became very familiar with his voice, but the first time I saw him in person, I was surprised at his size. That terrific sounding, deep voice was coming out of this little body? It didn't seem right. But Al had a terrific personality. He was a very personable and knowledgeable sports guy. But he wasn't the Suns' first play-by-play announcer. We went through a couple of guys before Al was hired. But after he was offered the job, the rest of the story is—he's still there!

> That terrific sounding, deep voice was coming out of this little body?

I don't think anyone realizes or recognizes an upcoming "legend" distinction. That just happens. The one thing I'll say about Al is that he probably was the greatest salesman for the game of basketball in our entire state. His voice was so well known. It became synonymous with the Phoenix Suns. He had as much to do with the success of the Suns as any player, coach, or manager...or all of us combined. He played that significant a role. My attitude was that he was always going to be there as long as I was.

Al McCoy is also an accomplished pianist and loves jazz. Al and I spent many a night on the road in restaurants and piano bars. We always enjoyed sharing a good meal, a glass of wine, and good conversation. He's a terrific guy, entertaining, and fun to be with. Al is not a complainer. He's a very, very positive guy and as professional today as he was when I first met him almost 40 years ago.

My attitude has always been, with anyone who is associated with me, that if something better came along, and someone wanted to go, that I would never hold anyone back, but I have seldom ever had anyone leave. They love being where they are. We have a family, and Al was a big part of that success story. I give Al all the glory possible for his many contributions to the Suns and professional sports. He's been a great ambassador for the game, the broadcast profession, and for the entire state.

Not many people know that I went to high school with Jim Bouton. Jim's father was transferred from New Jersey to Chicago while Jim was in high school. Jim wrote *Ball Four* and had some great years with the **YANKEES***. Jim and I were together last year at a big reunion in Chicago—the two of us emceed our high school reunion in 2008. Over the years, he visited me in Phoenix a few times and sat with me at some Diamondbacks games. Thinking

---

*Thomas Edison sold the concrete to the **YANKEES** that was used to build Yankee Stadium. Edison owned the huge Portland Cement Company...Edison's middle name was Alva, named after the father of onetime Cleveland Indians owner, Alva Bradley.

back to the day when we were awarded the baseball franchise, I was in **MIAMI***, Florida, at The Breakers. I was being interviewed by the press after we were awarded the team and who walks through the lobby and comes over to say hello? Jimmy. Small world.

When I got out of high school, I had 66 college basketball offers from schools of all sizes. Supposedly, at least a number of them said that I was considered the quickest white guy in the country. I was a shooter. I had limited my interest in schools to four: Illinois, because of home state; Notre Dame, because I always followed Notre Dame and the Italian Catholic community pushed me; Michigan, because I liked Michigan; and Kansas, because of Wilt Chamberlain. I chose Kansas, because I thought we could win an NCAA championship. Freshmen were not eligible to play varsity then.

As a sophomore, I knew I would start, because their guards couldn't shoot a lick. The way teams were defending Chamberlain, I knew I'd get plenty of shots. Bob Billings was one of the starting guards. Ron Loneski, a lefty, was there, as well as Monte Johnson. Bill Bridges and I played on the same freshman team. Suddenly, one night during that first semester, Wilt tells me he's leaving KU to sign with the **HARLEM GLOBETROTTERS***. He quit and got 75 grand. I immediately called the coach at Illinois, put my tail between my legs and headed home.

A few years later, in 1969, I'm coaching the Suns, our second year as a team, and we are playing the Lakers in the playoffs—yes, we made the playoffs in just our second year—and we have the Lakers

---

*Do you confuse Miami (Ohio) with **MIAMI** (Florida)? Miami of Ohio was a school before Florida was a state.

---

*BOB GIBSON played basketball with the Harlem Globetrotters several off-seasons....In 1972, Bill Cosby signed a lifetime contract with the Globetrotters for one dollar per year. In 1986, the Globetrotters gave him a nickel raise. Cosby made several appearances with the team and is an honorary member of the Basketball Hall of Fame.

down three games to one. They had West, Baylor and Chamber-lain at that time. I had Van Arsdale, Goodrich, Silas and Hawkins on the Suns. They come back and beat us, and it was Wilt who helped beat us in Game 7. That's the second time he got me.

But the one that hurt most of all was when he scored his 25,000th point in Phoenix, and I had to present him with the game ball.

Chapter 5

OF MIKES & MEN

From Hot Rod to Tiny Tim

IT WAS A BALL!

Hot Rod Hundley

Hot Rod Hundley was a flamboyant All-America guard from West Virginia who played his entire NBA career with the Lakers. He played from 1957 through 1963, with the first three years in Minneapolis and his last three years in Los Angeles. He began his broadcasting career as an analyst working alongside legendary Lakers broadcaster Chick Hearn. From there he joined the Suns broadcast team for a few years, before joining the Jazz as their play-by-play man. He retired at the end of last season after a 35-year run with the Jazz.

I started out working with Chick Hearn of the Lakers for two seasons. But I said to myself, "I want to do play-by-play. I don't want to be an analyst all of my life, and if I stay here, I'll always be an analyst." That turned out to be true. Chick lived to be 85 and was in L.A. for 42 years. The Phoenix Suns got a franchise while I was in L.A., and I talked to them and moved to Phoenix. The same thing happened when I left Phoenix and went down to New Orleans. I stayed with the Jazz all the way... for 35 years.

Al was a big part of the Suns' success and still is. He's a great friend and great broadcaster. If you couldn't see Al, you would think he was 7'5" and weighed 300 pounds, because of that voice he has. But here's this little guy with a great set of pipes. They love him down there in Phoenix. He has an unbelievable following. I don't know anyone who doesn't like Al McCoy. He got into the Basketball Hall of Fame as a broadcaster and deserved it, too. He's just an outstanding broadcaster.

I was with the Suns beginning with their second year in 1969–70. Bob Vache was the Suns' first play-by-play guy and was very big in Arizona at the time. He was a popular, good-looking guy and a little older than me. I was the analyst. One night the entire organization went to a big party to mingle with all the Suns' sponsors. When it was getting late, I didn't even notice that Bob had taken off. I went home and went to bed. A few hours later, I'll never forget it, the phone rang, and it was Jerry Colangelo. He said, "Did you hear about Vache? He just got killed in an accident." Vache was in a small car and he was killed on his way home.

We had a game the next night, and Jerry said, "Can you do play-by-play?" I said, "I'll tell you after the game!" I had never done it before. I remember that Dick Van Arsdale got the opening tip and I made it sound like the Suns just won the World Championship! By halftime I was so hoarse, I couldn't even talk.

Colangelo tells me to this day that he never thought my voice could hold up, or he would have given me the job. Joe McConnell did the Suns play-by-play for a year, and then along came Al McCoy. Al had been doing the play-by-play for the Roadrunners hockey team, and sometimes he'd come into my bar, The Court Jester, up on North Central. When Al got the Suns job, I was happy for him and looked forward to working with a good guy. He was just great, and he played off me. He let me do what I wanted to do and wasn't one of those guys who always hogged the microphone.

Some friends of mine were in the restaurant business, and they coached me with the Court Jester. It was a very small cocktail bar, and we had hamburgers and cheeseburgers. It would close at about 8 p.m. unless someone was in there. After every Suns game though, we would stay open until midnight, because the fans would come in.

Anyway, Al would come in there after games, along with a lot of players like Hawk and Dick Van Arsdale. It was good. They got everything in the house half off—all the players and the front office guys too. I had the Court Jester about five years. I had a great time and met a lot of people. It was a fun place.

Al McCoy and Chick Hearn were very much alike in their enthusiastic approach and both shared a real love for the game. You turn on the radio and listen to some broadcasters, and they're just talking...no oomph. But not Al and Chick. Their enthusiasm wasn't reserved just for when their teams were winning either. They never let it get down. I've always felt that way. They'd ride their enthusiasm for the whole game. They'd even give credit to the other team when their team was getting beat.

I left Phoenix in 1974. That was my last year with the Suns. In July, I was on my way to New Orleans. From New Orleans, it was on to Salt Lake City.

One night, Larry Miller, the owner of the Jazz, was standing outside the dressing room as the Suns came in for a game. I walked in with Al McCoy, and he runs up to Miller and starts reaming him out about putting the broadcasters up at the top of the building. Al said, "I'll tell you what, Larry, I don't agree with this." I cautioned Al, "You could get your butt fired!" He shot back, "I don't care. I'm standing up for my guys."

Larry didn't get ruffled by it. He told Al the reasoning. It's a money game, and we could sell those seats. Now every team is doing it. In Utah, I had one of the highest broadcast positions in the game. I'd turn around to fans behind me, offer them my binoculars and say, "Do you guys want to borrow these?"

Al's right. It's terrible from upstairs. We make mistakes. On the floor you would never miss a beat. We'd fly with it. Now you go upstairs, and it's a different way of broadcasting. Of course, Al is fighting for every broadcaster in the NBA. He's our director of basketball operations as far as the broadcasters are concerned. He'd put the radio guys in the front row and the TV guys in the second row. How 'bout that?

A COACH IS A TEACHER...
WITH A DEATH WISH

Vinnie Del Negro

Vinnie Del Negro had a 14-year career in pro basketball, with two years in Italy and 12 seasons in the NBA. Vinnie grew up in the birthplace of basketball... Springfield, Massachusetts and matriculated at North Carolina State. In addition to his two seasons in Phoenix, he played for four other NBA teams including Sacramento, San Antonio, Milwaukee and Golden State. For three years he was part of the Suns broadcast team as an analyst and two of those he spent sitting next to Al McCoy. He moved into the Suns front office dealing with player personnel, before he left the Suns to take over the head coaching duties for the Chicago Bulls.

When I retired as a player after 14 years, I got into television and did radio with Al for a couple of years. The best way for me to describe the experience was that Al made it easy for me. He could do games blindfolded. He doesn't need a script or note cards. All of his famous sayings, like S*hazam!*, are part of the passion and loyalty that he displays with his profession and the Suns organization. His talent and ability are unmatched.

In every arena we went into, Al knew all the electronic media guys. Al is like the mayor of every arena—they've known him so long. For me to work with Al was easy. It was fun, and you knew you were working with the best. Al made it that much more interesting to do the games. We had a lot of fun, whether on the plane, the sideline, or at dinner. You always want to play or work with the best people. I was fortunate because you'd be hard-pressed to find anybody that can do it any better than Al.

The Suns' dedication of their press room as the Al McCoy Media Center was a fitting tribute. It shows the history of Al's life and all the people he has been able to touch by what he loves to do, whether it's with his piano playing or his broadcasting. I remember going to Italy, and one of our owners had a birthday party on top of one of the buildings. There was a piano there, and Al played for a couple of hours. Everybody just loved it.

> **Al is like the mayor of every arena...**

He has great passion. Look at the media room displays, and you'll see not only players, coaches, fans, and people from his Iowa days, but also some pictures from his time in baseball. With all the basketball memories on those walls, he's taken a pretty interesting path from where he started.

When I'd go around the league, some of the other TV and radio guys would look at me and say *Shazam!* or some of his other little sayings. It shows you all of the people who watch the NBA and follow Suns games, because of Al. His presentation of the game is unique.

One of my jobs as an analyst was to interview the assistant coaches or other personnel. I handed the mike to Al after that, and he got the tape ready for the beginning of the game. The play-by-play guy is also the setup guy. It was an easy process with Al because his setups were so easy to blend into. It sounds easy to do, but with the speed of the game and reaction times, the flow of the game is very important. Al has a way—because it's almost second nature to him now—of ensuring that his setups and timing are right on cue. I only had to talk about basketball. Al knew that, and that's what he did to help me and the broadcast.

IF A BASKETBALL COULD TALK, IT WOULD SOUND LIKE AL MCCOY

Tom Ambrose

Tom Ambrose has been part of the Phoenix Suns organization for 37 years. He started in 1973 as the team's director of public relations and served in that capacity for 17 years. In 1987 he became senior vice president with responsibility for both public and community relations. He helped create Phoenix Suns Charities, the team's non-profit foundation and served as its executive director for 17 of its 21 years of existence. His current assignment with the team is in the community relations department.

I moved out to Arizona in 1971 from New Rochelle, New York, to marry my college sweetheart, a year after I graduated from Notre Dame. I packed all my worldly possessions in a trunk and flew out to Tucson, where my future wife's father had just taken a new job and moved the family. I had visited Phoenix a couple of times, and I was very excited about moving there, so Tucson was a last minute change. But in my infinite New York wisdom, I said, "What could possibly be the difference between Phoenix and Tucson? They're only 100 miles apart!"

I moved to Tucson and started going to graduate school in business at the University of Arizona. I finally decided I didn't want to do that anymore and started looking for a job in the Phoenix area in public relations. I had a little knowledge of the NBA, because one of my best buddies in high school was John Borgia, son of NBA ref Sid Borgia. I'd heard lots of NBA stories from the Borgias. I gave it a shot and wrote a letter to the GM of the Suns, Jerry Colangelo. He was nice enough to respond, and although he had no openings on his staff, he invited me to stop by the office the next time I was in Phoenix. Meanwhile, I was going through normal channels, what they now call "networking." Back then it was called "who do you know?"

I ended up talking to Dick Stewart, who worked for a PR firm called Jennings and Thompson. A week after I talked to him, he called me and said, "There's a guy named Bill Shover at Phoenix Newspapers and they've got a job opening for an entry level PR guy. You'd be perfect for it. Give him a call." I called Shover, and made an appointment to see him at two o'clock in the afternoon. I had to drive up from Tucson for the meeting, so I decided to see if I could get something going with this other guy I didn't know, Colangelo, on the same day. I called his office and said, "I'm going to be in Phoenix, and Jerry had written a letter to me inviting me to stop by. I'd like to set up a time to see him. Maybe eleven o'clock?" His administrative assistant said, "Sure. Come on in."

At eleven o'clock, I go in to see Colangelo. Following the usual get-to-know-you chat, he said, "I like your story, but I don't have anything for you right now. Something may open up down the road, but I can't be sure. Who else are you talking to in town?" I said, "I'm scheduled to meet with Bill Shover at two o'clock." He just shakes his head and laughs. I said, "What's so funny?" He said, "I am leaving you here. I'm going to drive down to Phoenix Newspapers and pick up Bill Shover for lunch. I'll put in a good word for you." I said, "You will?" He said, "Yeah, sure, absolutely."

Years later, Jerry tells the story this way: "I talked to Shover and said, 'Look, here's this kid. He seems good, but he needs some experience. I want the right to call him up if I need him.'" I always say to Jerry, "However you want to tell that story is fine with me, because it's worked out beautifully." I went to work for Shover for about a year-and-a-half, doing entry level PR, and then Colangelo called me up to the "bigs."

I was relating that story to a friend who made me realize how incredible that day was almost 40 years ago. He said, "Are you kidding me? You just walked in and saw two of the most powerful people in the city of Phoenix in the same day!" No big deal. I just thought there was a guardian angel sitting on my shoulder.

Years later, the Suns had defeated Rick Barry and the defending champion Golden State Warriors in the 1976 Western Conference Finals and it was on to the NBA Finals to take on the Boston Celtics. The Celtics won the first two games in Boston, but the Suns bounced back with two big wins at the Coliseum. So it was 2–2 going back to Boston for a pivotal Game Five. Rick Barry joined the CBS TV crew to help with color commentary, along with Mendy Rudolph, a former NBA referee. Barry had a tough time. He constantly referred to Paul Westphal as Paul West*field* throughout the playoff series. The play-by-play man was **BRENT MUSBURGER***. Game 5, because of the CBS broadcast, started at 9 p.m., Boston time. It was a Friday night. Al McCoy and I speculated as to where everybody went between the time they got off work at five o'clock in Boston and four hours later when the game started. Let's just say that there was a real buzz in the building at tip-off.

The broadcast position for Suns radio was in a little press box on the leading edge of the upper deck of the old Boston Garden. It was a great vantage point, except you couldn't hear some of the calls or see things that were going on close to the court. In order to get in and out of this little press box there was a step or two that led up into the regular seats and then back up to the exit-way.

Several guys had gotten tickets right next to Al and me…or maybe they just moved down from higher seats and took up residence on the press box steps. They continued what they had started at five o'clock and were drinking pretty heavily throughout the whole game. At one point they offered Al a drink…naturally he refused. The Suns go down by 22 in the first half and it looks like

***BRENT MUSBURGER** was the home plate umpire when Tim McCarver made his pro baseball debut for Keokuk, Iowa, in the Midwest League in 1959.

it's pretty well over for Phoenix, but the Suns slowly mount a comeback, and by the end of regulation, the game is tied.

Just before the end of regulation, Al realized these guys were getting a little unruly, so he asked me to go up and get a security guard. I climbed back up 10 rows or so and found the security guard standing there yakking to an usher about the game. I said, "Hey, guys, we've got a couple of people sitting in the press box, and we'd like to get them out of there." The cop looked at me and said, "What? Are they bothering you?" I said, "No, not exactly. But they're not supposed to be there. It could be a problem." He just waved me off. "Yeah, yeah, yeah, we'll take care of it."

I went back to my duties of keeping score and doing the occasional on-air scoring summaries for Al, but that was it. Security never got around to helping us. Meanwhile, the game goes into overtime...and then an amazing second overtime. Then, **JOHN HAVLICEK*** hit a leaping leaner to put the Celtics up by one as time ran out. The crowd stormed the floor, and there was a fight between referee Richie Powers and one of the Boston fans right out in the middle of the floor. I guess someone was a little unhappy with the officiating that night. A couple of Suns players, Curtis Perry and Dennis Awtrey, were trying to break up the fight. It was absolute bedlam on the court below us! Al was looking at the scoreboard, because he thought there was still time left. Eventually, order was restored, and it was Suns ball with one second left. Paul Westphal, realizing that the odds of the Suns going the length of the court and scoring was less than nil, convinced Coach MacLeod to call a timeout even though the Suns had none left. That resulted in a technical foul, which the Celtics' Jo Jo White converted, but the maneuver gave the ball to the Suns at center court, now down by two with one second to play.

---

*Late hamburger king Dave Thomas named the company after his daughter, Wendy. Wendy was once a babysitter for **JOHN HAVLICEK**'s children.

The Suns inbounded the ball to Gar Heard at the top of the key, and he launched a high arching jumper—the shot heard around the world—that swished through cleanly at the buzzer! At that moment, one of the two inebriates sitting right next to us passed out, right onto Al McCoy's lap! As Al was calling what is arguably the most exciting play in Phoenix Suns history, there was a drunk passed out in his lap! Al deftly pushed him off his lap and down into a pile at the foot of the stairs.

There's an old record album somewhere of the exciting play-by-play from late in that second overtime. All of a sudden, you hear this high-pitched, squeaky voice say, "There's a fight out on the floor!" Because Al was looking for the clock and trying to figure out what was going on with the time, he was looking down at the official timer and up at the scoreboard clock. He did not see the fight on the court. So, I had an open

> ...one of the two inebriates sitting right next to us passed out, right onto Al McCoy's lap!

mike, and I just jumped in, and that was my five seconds of fame. It's on this record album, and I'm sure a lot of people who listen to the recording say, "Who the heck is that?"

The media room was something that Suns' management really wanted to do for Al before he retired and while he was still a big part of the organization. It was done at the behest of owner Robert Sarver and Rick Welts, our team president. Alvan Adams and I were assigned to pulling the project together and getting it done. We spent a while collecting some copy and getting a timeline together.

Then we started working with a team from Campbell Fisher. Those guys are the designers. To create the Al McCoy Media Center, we worked on the copy, and Alvan worked on a possible layout for what used to be called the press room. On the walls are many photos, and a timeline of Al's life and career wraps around the room. On one column, we have a transcribed version of Al's play-by-play from that famous Game 5 in Boston Garden from the 1976 NBA Finals. We put it into a graphic that wraps around the column. If you want the play-by-play from the critical moments in that game when Gar Heard hit his "shot heard 'round the world," you can walk around that pillar several times and read the whole thing.

The rest of the room is a real tribute to Al and his life. Many broadcasters from around the NBA submitted words of encouragement and respect for Al. We were pleased with the outcome, and I think Al is very proud of it. The best part was when we had the ribbon-cutting opening ceremony. We had a video retrospective of Al's life. Then we walked over and cut the ribbon on the new Al McCoy room. It was very exciting. This was in June 2008. It's been up for a while, and everybody, particularly all the visiting broadcasters and people who come into town, think it's a great tribute and one that is certainly well deserved by Al.

It was so surprising to me, as we put all this together, that Al still looks pretty much like he looked when he was 10 years old. There was one youthful picture in particular where he just looks like a kid who would get into a lot of mischief, like the Mugs McGinnis character from the old Bowery Boys TV serial.

Al McCoy is a total broadcasting professional with amazing talent. Over the years, every time we had to do a public service announcement or a 30-second commercial for the Suns, Al would read over the copy once and then, on his first take, nail it at 29.5 seconds. It was uncanny. He's done that throughout his career. He seems to have a clock in his head. He knows how fast or how slow he has to read to bring the spot in on time. It's rare when Al does more than two takes on a spot.

WORKING WITH AL MCCOY IS LIKE PLAYING HOOKY FROM LIFE

Tim Kempton

Tim Kempton graduated from the University of Notre Dame and was selected in the sixth round of the 1986 NBA Draft by the L.A. Clippers. He went on to have an eight-year NBA career with the Clippers, Hornets, Nuggets, Suns, Cavs, Hawks, Spurs and Raptors. He was a member of the 1992-93 Suns team that won 62 games and advanced to the NBA Finals. He is now in his seventh year working with Al McCoy and providing color commentary on Suns radio broadcasts.

I get to work with a Hall of Famer. You don't usually get the opportunity to work with someone who is regarded as the best in the business, as your first assignment. From that standpoint, it's been phenomenal.

Seven years ago, I went on the road with the Suns for a preseason game against Portland, to see if Al and I could get along and work together. I did that game, came home, and Al said, "Would you like to do it?" I said, "Sure!" It was quick and out of the blue. Getting into radio broadcasting wasn't anything that was planned on my part, but it's been a great experience. As we travel around the country, I get to meet everyone Al has ever worked with, like Hot Rod Hundley and Dick Van Arsdale. Also knowing JoAnn and Cotton Fitzsimmons and the rest of the guys, I'm constantly hearing stories about the early days of Al McCoy on the road with Joe Proski. There's hardly a city we visit where Al hasn't played the piano at a hotel or at a piano bar down the street.

The interesting thing is that everybody told me in the beginning, "You did so well right off the bat." It was actually pretty straightforward. Al would sit there with his finger ready, and he would just point to me to let me know when to speak. Everyone made fun of it, and I said, "You know what? It was the best thing in the world. I knew when it was coming. It wasn't something blind. Al would let me know when my time was coming up and I just followed his lead."

> Cotton's wife, JoAnn, still sits right behind us at every home game.

This gig has been an incredibly lucky break. I did not do any communications work in college. It wasn't something I thought about, but in the long run, it worked out. I started out with Tom Leander. He called me in to do some pregame and halftime stuff. I did about 10 to 15 games that year with him, which led to doing Phoenix Mercury games, which, in turn, led to doing TV for ASU men's basketball. ASU's athletic director at the time was Gene Smith. Gene played football at my alma mater, Notre Dame. I'm sure that was part of what led to doing radio with Al. I wound up doing the whole season. I broke in the easy way. At the beginning, everything I did was on the road, so the easy part was picking up the home schedule after I had been traveling all the time. Cotton was still well enough to do the home games, but when he passed away, I picked up the whole schedule.

Al and Cotton were extremely close. Cotton's wife, JoAnn, still sits right behind us at every home game. She's literally 10 feet away from us, so we still get to see her quite a bit. It was difficult stepping in after Cotton, because those two guys were so close and had such a good relationship. That's what the tryout was all about. Al is phenomenal. He's still the best at calling the game up and down the court and that's why it's been so easy for me. I've been working for a Hall of Famer. There were many times when he made me look extremely good, especially early on.

Al loves to talk about his roots in Iowa. If there are any Iowa kids on the opposing team's roster, he makes it a point to go and talk to them and bring up their hometown roots. He loves Iowa, Iowa basketball and Drake basketball in particular. It's a lot of fun. He takes a lot of pride in what he does.

My college roommate was Skip Holtz, **LOU HOLTZ**'s* son. It was phenomenal. I was introduced to Lou in a very different way. He was my roommate's dad as opposed to Lou Holtz, the football coach. The first time I met him was at the Holtz's family dinner table as opposed to a locker room. That was unique. I followed Skip around. I went down to Florida State to hang out when he was with **BOBBY BOWDEN***. When he was with Earle Bruce at Colorado State, learning the running game, I hung out there, too. When Skip went back to Notre Dame, I'd hang out in the summer with him. It was a neat experience. Lou was someone who "got it." He realized it was all about Notre Dame. You were a part of Notre Dame. Notre Dame wasn't a part of you. Charlie Weis thinks it's all about him, which to me it isn't what it is.

*When **LOU HOLTZ** was coaching Arkansas, his personal attorney was Bill Clinton.

*During his long career, Florida State coach **BOBBY BOWDEN**, was offered the head coaching jobs at Marshall University and LSU. Bowden eventually turned down both opportunities...the two coaches that accepted those positions were both killed in job-related plane crashes.

IF YOU'RE LUCKY ENOUGH TO WORK WITH AL MCCOY, YOU'RE LUCKY ENOUGH

Keith Erickson

Keith Erickson was a 6'5" forward who played under John Wooden at UCLA. Drafted by San Francisco in 1965, he played one season there before he was traded to Chicago. Two years in Chicago were followed by five seasons with the L.A. Lakers. Erickson came to the Suns in a controversial deal for Connie Hawkins and put in four solid years in a Suns uniform. He worked as a color commentator on Lakers broadcasts with Chick Hearn and later on Suns games with Al McCoy.

I began working with Al McCoy on the Suns' broadcasts during the 1998–'99 season. I had some national broadcasting experience with CBS. Then I broadcast with the Lakers for seven years, working with Chick Hearn, who is without a doubt, the toughest guy to work with. Chick always believed that the entire broadcast was his. The color commentators didn't say anything until Chick took a breath. By the time he blew his breath out, you had to be off. I spent seven years working with Chick, so I knew what working with a tough broadcaster was like. Working with Al was a piece of cake.

I started off in Phoenix working with Gary Bender for a couple of years on TV. We had been really good friends. When I teamed up with Al, the mistake I used to make all the time, and it made my heart drop every time I did it, was calling Al... *Gary.* I was so used to saying, "That's right, Gary," or "Thanks, Gary," that I made the mistake too many times. I felt awful every time I did it, but I did it right up to the last season I was with him. Al was always great about it. Also, every now and then, when Al wasn't quite through, I would "step" on him. I felt badly about those kinds of things. Al was such a good guy and such a professional. Everybody in Phoenix loved him. I can't believe that he's not doing the television broadcast right now. He's been doing it for so long—he *is* the Voice of the Suns.

Al is similar to Chick in that their voices are so outstanding, so distinctive. Chick had a built-in excitement for the game and so does Al. He knows when to raise it and when to back off. He's just the ultimate professional, as Chick was. Chick taught Southern California the game of professional basketball. He'd been broadcasting Lakers games since 1961. Al did the same thing with the Suns in Phoenix, coming in after a couple of other guys had briefly done it. He's the one everybody remembers.

I had a great time playing in Phoenix, especially that year we went to the NBA Finals and played the triple overtime game in Boston Garden. We had a great group of guys.

I had played for the Lakers prior to that, with Jerry West, Elgin Baylor, and Wilt Chamberlain. There have never been three greater players than those guys. It was a completely different situation in Phoenix with Paul Westphal and Alvan Adams as the best players on that team.

> He knows when to raise it and when to back off. He's just the ultimate professional.

In Phoenix, we had to be more of a team, which made it that much more fun. Today, there's all the dunking and the flashy play, as opposed to just getting it done like a John Stockton would have—the way Coach John Wooden taught the game, which was the best way.

COTTON FITZSIMMONS WAS GOD'S WAY OF BEING NICE TO PHOENIX

JoAnn Fitzsimmons

JoAnn Fitzsimmons is the widow of the late Lowell "Cotton" Fitzsimmons. During Cotton's second stint as coach of the Suns (1988-1992), JoAnn organized the Suns wives into a hard-working group that provided great support for the team foundation, Phoenix Suns Charities. She remains on the PSC board today and attends every Suns game, sitting just a few feet away from Al McCoy's broadcast location.

I'm obviously biased, because Cotton was my husband. There's a saying that when someone dies, people always say nice things about them. The best thing anybody said to me after Cotton passed away was when Al McCoy told me, "But people always said nice things about Cotton when he was alive."

We act differently around different people. When you're around your close friends, your guard is down, and you are a little more natural than if you were having lunch with Jerry Colangelo or the president of some big corporation. The thing that endeared people to Cotton so much was that he acted the same whether he was playing golf with a big politician or with a friend like Tom Ambrose. His conversation was the same. While they may not always have agreed with him, they at least respected his total honesty. He was always the same no matter whose company he was in, whether he was alone with me or having lunch with Senator Jon Kyl.

A lot of people, when they get fired or things don't work out, burn bridges—there are bad feelings. Cotton always looked at it as business and not something personal. When he took the job in San Antonio, we went out to dinner with the owner and the general manager after the press conference. That night, Cotton said to owner Angelo Drossos, "You know, one of these days, you're probably going to fire me, and I just want to make sure that we handle it the same way as you hiring me. I don't want any bad feelings. We'll go out to dinner. We'll have a bottle of wine. We'll have a toast to both of our futures." Angelo said, "Oh, Cotton, that's crazy. I would never fire you." Cotton said, "Listen, I understand this business. You can't get rid of the team. The coach has to take the blame, and I'm willing to do that." When they did fire him in San Antonio, that's exactly what we did. Cotton had traded George Gervin, and everything was in disarray in San Antonio. We went out that night with Angelo and, of course, all the people in the restaurant were looking at us in a most peculiar way. Cotton said that was not something most people do.

Did anybody else ever refer to Al as *Big Al*? I don't know whether this was something unique to Cotton and Al, or if lots of people called Al that. Cotton always did. Maybe it had to do with the fact that they were both small, or perhaps it was a sign of respect, but Cotton always referred to him as Big Al.

Cotton and Al were relatively short in stature, yet neither one of them had a problem getting respect from the players who towered over them. You could see Cotton pulling on the jersey of a player that was seven-feet tall to get his attention. Cotton was strong and certainly took control of every situation he was in. Al is the same way.

Cotton and Al had this relationship for so long. When Cotton was here with the Suns for the first time in 1970, Al wasn't with the Suns yet. Al came to work for the Suns after Cotton left in '72. They had met, and Cotton would always say that he told Jerry before he left, "You need to hire that Al McCoy. He's got a great voice." Somehow, even though they didn't work together, they developed a friendship.

> Cotton didn't have broadcast experience when he went on the air with Al, but he could talk!

When we were in Kansas City in the '70s and '80s, it was a totally different era. There were no charter planes. Everybody was from the old school. Wives didn't go on any trips, and yet, Cotton, Al, and Joe Proski were such good friends that if the Suns were coming to play in Kansas City, and they had more than a day there, or if it happened to be over a weekend, Jan Proski and Georgia McCoy would come to Kansas City, and the six of us would just have the best time. That was really a wonderful thing, and we were friends for so many years, even being on different teams. Then, it got that much better when Cotton came back to Phoenix.

When Al and Georgia would visit Kansas City, we would do Kansas City stuff. We'd just hang out together. They'd come out to our house or, since Cotton and Al were big on having their favorite restaurants in every city, we'd go down to a steakhouse in Kansas City or the Plaza III down at the Country Club Plaza. Al knew all the best restaurants in every city.

Cotton didn't have broadcast experience when he went on the air with Al, but he could talk! Everybody always teased him about that. Cotton always deferred to Al. When they were doing stuff, even if he had something to say, he would never interrupt Al. He would wait for Al's signal. When they were on the radio, no one could see him, and Al would point to him or give him a signal. He would jump in only when Al gave him the signal, because he had that much respect for him. He knew that Al knew what he was doing and was, after all, the Voice of the Suns. Cotton wasn't going to be interrupting and talking. That had to do with the respect Al and Cotton had for each other. He thought Al was the best.

From the time Al and Cotton met, they had so much in common—their small-town Midwestern roots, the fact that they both were circle-breakers in their communities, and the success they came to enjoy in the NBA. They both broke out of that small-town Midwestern life. The other commonality was their personalities. They were so much alike in terms of how they treated people. Al is such a goodwill ambassador for the Suns. He's out in public all the time. He's in restaurants, and he talks and mingles with people. That's why the fans love Al so much. They feel like they know him personally, because he never puts up a wall.

Cotton would always say, "That's the way Midwesterners are." He would always tease me and say, "I know New Yorkers aren't like that, but that's the way Midwesterners are." I could see Al McCoy doing the exact same thing.

I have fabulous memories. Al does, too. I am so happy that I was around during that time in the NBA, when we really had so much fun. Cotton and Al had this 30-year relationship. Nobody has that anymore. There's no chance of that happening, because people surround themselves with their own people. They don't come in to form relationships with people on the team or in the town they come to. They bring all their friends with them. We have lifelong relationships with people from the time he came into the NBA, and it's the same with Al. Al has relationships with people in every city he's gone to. People don't do that anymore. Al would go out in every city he traveled to. He would look up people he knew there and meet them for dinner if he had a night off. Most people now order room service and stay in their rooms.

THE WRITE GUY

Joe Gilmartin

Joe Gilmartin was a sports columnist for the Phoenix Gazette for more than 30 years. He was also the first president of the Pro Basketball Writers Association of America. Gilmartin joined the Gazette as assistant sports editor in 1962 after working in Wichita, Kan. He was named sports editor in 1973 and held the post until 1991. Since retiring from Phoenix Newspapers in 1996, he has been writing for the Suns' and Diamondbacks' Web sites. Gilmartin wrote the 1976 book, The Little Team That Could...And Darn Near Did —*recounting the Suns' first trip to the NBA Finals. Gilmartin covered 25 NBA Finals, 15 Final Fours, 20 Super Bowls and 14 World Series.*

I was one of Al's broadcast partners for some years. The Suns were looking for an analyst, and I had covered the NBA for a hundred years, so they asked me to do it. We did it on cable and on radio for six or seven years, maybe longer. It was a real treat working next to Al. Sometimes you don't get a full appreciation for the job announcers do. People talk a lot about style--some people like one person's style and some like another.

The thing that impressed me from the start about Al was how extremely well-prepared and conscientious he was. As the years went on, I was also impressed with the fact that no matter what the game was—and believe me, there were some miserable games during those years—he never seemed to lose his enthusiasm. I'd be falling asleep at the table, and Al would still be into the game. He's just very good at what he does. Basketball is not an ideal radio game, to be honest with you. It drives me crazy, but Al is one of a handful of people who does it very well. One of the keys to his success is his ability to stay on top of the action.

I traveled with Al for many years. In the earlier days when we were together, he didn't have an engineer. He had to do it himself. We were in New York once, and he needed a chair. Of course, New York is a union town. The guy who was in charge of chairs in New York was off duty and *they couldn't get him a chair*! Al could get very upset at times. We finally worked something out, but it wasn't easy. Al thought we could just go get a chair, but that's not the way it works with unions.

When Al first started broadcasting games, the NBA wasn't going that well. As a matter of fact, it wasn't that many years ago that the NBA had to pay to have their games on the air. It was not like it is now. Pro basketball was almost an afterthought. It was a niche sport—it wasn't mainstream at all. In those earlier days, the NBA played games all over the place, not just in NBA cities. It wasn't quite as elaborate in the telecasting, and there were a lot of things we had to improvise. I remember having some technical difficulties during a game once, and Al had to broadcast from a phone booth for a while.

I do remember one time we were doing a game in Buffalo. All of a sudden, they empty the building. Everybody starts leaving. Al is broadcasting, and I'm analyzing up a storm. The arena was located right next to their courthouse. There had been a bomb at the courthouse earlier that week that they ended up finding in time. Now, another bomb threat had been phoned in. I looked around and said to Al, "Al, how come we're the only ones left in this building? Do they know something we don't?" They finally brought all the people back in, and we finished the game.

In his heart, Al would really have liked to have also been a baseball announcer. Baseball's a radio game. He was a really close friend of Horace Stoneham. At one time, he came fairly close to broadcasting the Giants' games. He was a good announcer, regardless of the sport.

I came to work in Phoenix in 1961, writing for *The Phoenix Gazette.* I was the first president of the Pro Basketball Writers Association. The interesting thing about that is that I wasn't a member. We were in Chicago for the All-Star Game. There was a real character named Bob Logan, who unfortunately has since died, and I knew him pretty well. I was staying at the airport hotel. All of a sudden, there's a knock on the door. Pat says to me, "Good afternoon, Mr. President." They'd had this meeting to form the thing. The New York and Philadelphia factions were feuding like crazy, which is no big surprise. They couldn't agree on whom to make president, so I got the job. It was several years before I finally joined the organization.

> "They've awarded a franchise. Guess where?" They told him Phoenix, and he said, "You've got to be kidding."

I wasn't sure pro basketball would work *anywhere* at the beginning. If you get an NBA franchise today, you've got to guarantee millions of dollars and make all kinds of guarantees. You've got to have an arena. When Phoenix was awarded the franchise here, there was no advance warning. It was like we woke up one morning, and there was a basketball team on our front doorstep. I can't emphasize how small-potatoes the NBA was. It was nothing back then.

As for getting basketball in Phoenix, let me put it this way. Many people, New York's Ned Irish, for instance, and the guys in the East, were totally opposed to putting a basketball team here. Jerry Colangelo, who became the Godfather here of not only basketball, but everything else, too, had been offered a job in Seattle and had been talking to people there. He was in Seattle when somebody said to him, "They've awarded a franchise. Guess where?" They told him Phoenix, and he said, "You've got to be kidding."

THE SHU FITS...IN PHOENIX

John Shumate

After winning All-America honors at Notre Dame, John Shumate was a first round pick of the Suns in 1974, but he sat out what would have been his rookie year due to health issues. During that season, he joined Al McCoy courtside as part of the Suns broadcast team. Shumate returned to action the next season and had a five year NBA career with additional stops in Buffalo, Detroit, Houston, San Antonio and Seattle. Currently, he is an assistant coach with the Suns.

I'm one of the original sidekicks. I think Van Arsdale may have been *the* original Al McCoy sidekick. I'd never done any sort of broadcasting work. I couldn't play in 1974 because I had blood clotting problems. When they told me I couldn't play, I thought I was just going to have to sit out a year, but they said, "No. You're going to work with Al McCoy. He's absolutely the best in the business." So I said okay.

I remember going to the games and learning all of Al's little sayings and slogans: *the Flying Dutchman* and *Shu for two*. He was such a professional. He's the nicest and most professional person you'll ever be around. He's a tremendous basketball fan and a great fan of the athletes.

The thing that amazes me the most about Al is when you look at him you see this little, unobtrusive guy who wouldn't harm a fly, who you think would probably run if you said *boo*. Al's an inconspicuous package. If you are not careful when you open that package, you're going to run into a combination of Joe Frazier,

MUHAMMAD ALI*, Sugar Ray Leonard, Sugar Ray Robinson, Joe Louis, and Rocky Marciano all at once. He'll come out swinging, and he's a tough guy. He doesn't take any crap from anybody. He will tell you when to get on and when to get off. He doesn't care how big or tall you are. It absolutely doesn't matter to him who you are. If you open that package the wrong way, you could have some issues.

Al's a true friend. No matter where I've been—after I was traded by the Suns—whenever I saw Al on the road, he would always say, "Shu, let's go to dinner after the game." Or, when I came back to take a different role here, he would always come by my office and ask, "How's it going? Tell me what's going on. How are you doing?" Al was always concerned and always giving positive input, but he always—always—had those boxing gloves on and was ready to go.

One thing you don't do with Al is talk politics.

*In 1979 **MUHAMMAD ALI** beat NFL lineman Lyle Alzado in 8 rounds in an actual boxing match.

TAKE THIS JOB AND LOVE IT

Eddie Johnson

Eddie Johnson played 17 years in the NBA piling up 19,202 points, a career scoring average of 16.0. He is the NBA's all-time leading scorer among players with no All-Star appearances. A second round draft pick by Kansas City in 1981, he spent six seasons with the Kings before coming to the Suns in a trade in 1987. He played three-plus seasons for the Suns. One of best pure shooters in NBA history, "EJ" teaches shooting technique through clinics and videos. He is now in his 10th season as an analyst on the Suns broadcast team.

I came to the Suns in a trade in 1987, and I've now been involved with Al for 20 years. He's become almost like a father figure. Cotton Fitzsimmons was already like my surrogate father. I grew up in a single-parent household, so I valued the close relationship Cotton and I had. I learned a lot being around Al, Joe Proski, and Cotton—even as a player.

I can honestly say that just being around Al as a player, hearing his voice, seeing how knowledgeable he was about the game, how good he made the telecast sound, and then doing interviews with him after games, it really started to pique my interest in actually doing TV.

He probably wouldn't remember, but I used to ask him questions about what you had to do to get into radio and TV. He was always extremely nice to me. Then when the Suns hired me to work with him, he just made life so easy. He probably wouldn't take credit for it, but he really did. Doing simulcasts with him for four or five years, I learned a lot and really enjoyed working with him.

I used to give Al a hard time, because he was so direct in his telecasts. Even though he would ad-lib at times, he followed the same formula. One of the structures he developed with me was that as we're doing the game, he would point to me to let me know I could talk. You'd have to see it, but here I am watching the game, but I'm watching Al at the same time because I'm waiting for "the point," waiting for the signal so I can start talking. After a while, I never paid attention to him because I just knew when he was going to point.

> On the way to the game, I'm terrified I might actually have to do the game.

I've never seen a person do a telecast or radio as he does. I've done games with him where I thought there's no way he was going to be able to do the game. One of those times, he was sick and had his sunglasses on. We were on the road, so I knew they couldn't get a replacement for him. He looked at me, and I knew something was wrong. He said, "I don't know. You might have to do it all tonight." No way was I going to try to do a simulcast. Doing play-by-play is one of the hardest jobs. On the way to the game, I'm terrified I might actually have to do the game. I should have known better, because when we got there—and I don't know how he did it—he did the telecast. I'm telling you, he was really a basket case, but no one would ever have known.

The way he floats, it just makes it so easy for you to do your thing and blend in with him. He has had a number of analyst partners. Some play-by-play guys have a problem with that—they struggle. But Al didn't struggle.

CHICAGO'S CHOICE VOICE

Neil Funk

Neil Funk is now in his 19th season broadcasting Chicago Bulls basketball. Prior to joining the Bulls, Funk was the announcer for the Philadelphia 76ers for four seasons and won an Emmy award for his broadcasting in 1989. His first NBA stint was with Philadelphia in 1976-77 before he moved to Kansas City to do Kings games. He has also done play-by-play for the New Jersey Nets and the University of Illinois.

My first season in the NBA was 33 years ago, back in 1976–'77. Al was already well established with the Suns.

I started my NBA career in Philadelphia and stayed there for one year. Then I took a job with the Kansas City Kings doing their radio and television. The Kings were in the NBA's Western Conference in those days, so I saw quite a bit of Al. Kansas City, under the right ownership and maybe some deeper pockets, probably could have made it work there. But they sold the team to some people from Sacramento, and the handwriting was on the wall that they were going to move. They played another year or two in Kansas City after they were sold and then moved the franchise to Sacramento. By that time, I had gone back to Philadelphia.

I was new to this business, and Al had been doing it for awhile. Even in those days, Al was a mentor—I don't want to say father figure—as I was coming in and trying to figure out the NBA. He was always very cordial and made a point to come down to see how I was doing or if I needed anything. In our later years, probably the last 15 or so, we've become very close, and when one of us goes to the other's city, we always have lunch and dinner together.

HARRY CARAY* was bigger than life and out every night after the games, in every tavern in Chicago. I wouldn't consider Al to have that kind of personality. He's a fun-loving guy and loves to eat well and have a glass of wine. He's one of the funniest people I've ever been around. People wouldn't think that because he seems very serious, but he has a dry sense of humor. While I might be ticked off about something like seating in the arena or whatever the case might be, he has a way of turning it around so you aren't ticked off anymore. He makes you think it's funny!

> He's one of the funniest people I've ever been around.

Al's been around long enough and achieved enough that he doesn't have to sit in the back of the bus. If he doesn't care for someone, he pretty much makes his opinion known, whether it's another broadcaster or a coach. You just won't find many guys in the league as professional and caring as Al is. The thing that I always saw was that when the younger broadcasters came into the league, they'd gravitate to Al. It's incredible. They'll call him and ask him things. I've always taken the attitude of "Ah, let them do what they're doing!" But with Al, for some reason, they just call him. It's not like Al goes up to them and says to call him whenever they want. Every time I talk to Al he'll say, "Gosh, you won't believe who called me." They all feel that Al is a little bit of a father figure to them and has been around and knows what's going on in the league. They gravitate to him.

*In 1949, **HARRY CARAY**'s first wife Dorothy divorced him. In 1979 Harry wrote her: "Dearest Dorothy, Enclosed is my 360th alimony check. How much longer is this _ _ _ _ going to continue?" Dorothy responded: "Dearest Harry, Til death do us part. Love, Dorothy." Harry paid monthly till he passed away in Palm Springs in 1998.

In the early days, when we were simulcasting in Kansas City, it was me, myself and I. I didn't have a color guy. I was doing a simulcast on radio and television, plus carrying the equipment. I'm sure Al can relate to that. You had to carry the equipment, set it up, and crawl underneath the table to plug it in. After the game, you had to pack it up and lug it to the next arena. Do you really need a color guy? No. Does it make it a little easier? Definitely on the TV side. It's nice to have somebody for radio, but for my first seven or eight years in the league, I worked by myself.

Not too long ago, somebody calls me and says, "Hey! Would you mind if we set up a camera at the United Center in Chicago so you can say a few words about Al?" I called Al and told him, "I'm sick and tired of this. There is nothing left I can say about you!"

A COOL GUY IN HOTLANTA

Steve Holman

Steve Holman begins his 25th season behind the microphone on Atlanta Hawks radio. Holman had done play-by-play and color commentary on Hawks broadcasts for 3 1/2 years before taking over the full time play-by-play duties in 1989. Holman's first radio job was as a 17-year-old high school senior at WCCM, where he got to work under sportscasting icon Curt Gowdy, who owned the station. Holman has been involved in the NBA since the early 1970s when he was broadcast assistant to the Boston Celtics' late play-by-play legend Johnny Most.

I was just a Boston kid, 17 or 18 years old, when I started to work for Curt Gowdy. I did sports and news and used to hang around the studio. One of the guys got drafted when I was a junior in high school, so they put me on weekends on WCCM. The first thing I did was get a pass to go to all the Celtics games. I went and sat up by Johnny Most and introduced myself to him. As time went on, I would get his coffee and his English Ovals. He let me keep score for him. That's how I first met Al. In fact, I always remember Al because he was one of the guys who was really nice to me. A lot of times, guys don't have to be nice to kids like that. Al always said hello. He and Cleveland's Joe Tait were the two guys who didn't seem to care that you were just breaking in.

Al doesn't feel threatened by people. A lot of times, guys who aren't as good as Al are so worried that someone is going to take their job, they immediately try to find things wrong with people and try to give the appearance that they are better than everyone else. Al couldn't be more humble and nice. It was the same with Johnny Most. He was as nice as he could be to me as a kid and he took me under his wing. Joe Tait was another guy who did the same thing. Those old-timers were all nice. Al is one of my mentors, because of that.

When I first started doing games, no one could have been happier for me than Al. He helped me and showed me the ropes; told me all about the different arenas and where we sat. He gave me the ins and outs on PR people and engineers, who the good ones were and who you had to work with a little bit more. He gave me all the info. When we had our NBA broadcast meetings every year in New York, Al was terrific, because he and other guys like Neil Funk were the ringleaders of the announcers.

Al would arrange our dinners at the meetings. On the first night, the NBA would take us all out, and on another night we were on our own. Al was arranging this dinner, and everyone was going. A couple of guys from the NBA ended up having to go with us, because they didn't know what we were up to. Ha!

> **What Al is trying to do... is the right thing to do.**

What Al is trying to do by opposing the announcers moving up high is the right thing to do. I do believe it's inevitable that we are all going to get moved. Even Al knows that. But if no one said anything, we would probably just be moved farther and farther away. We know it's a money thing. They sell those courtside seats for $1,200 to $1,500 a game. I like to think of us as a two-and-a-half hour NBA infomercial—really! When I first broke in, that was the thing. Johnny Most taught me, "It's the good guys against the bad guys." That's the great thing about radio. Now all the games are pretty much on television, but there are still people who listen to the radio. People still tell me they turn the television sound down to listen to the radio.

When I go to Phoenix, Al takes me out to dinner, and whenever he comes here, I take him out. Al's probably the only guy left who does that. Charter flights have hurt the camaraderie that we used to have, because we always used to spend the night after a game. You'd be able to go out and meet the other announcer at the hotel and have a drink or two. Now everybody flies right out after games. There are still a few like Neil Funk, Al, and guys like that who try to make it work. As soon as the NBA schedule comes out in July, I usually get a call from Al, and we talk about our schedules. In Phoenix, we usually go to Donovan's on Camelback. He has his own booth there. The Hawks usually stay at the Ritz, so it's right down the street. There is a steakhouse in Atlanta called Bones where we like to go.

In New York, when we've been to NBA meetings, we've gone to several piano bars. He lives for piano bars and places that have jazz. He'll fill me in on all the places around the league, too. When we're on the road, he'll say, "Now you've got to go here and here and here..." He'll give me the names of places where they have music and that kind of entertainment. Guys don't even really go out to dinner like they used to on the road.

I went to Al's **HALL OF FAME*** induction. It was great. I was just like one of his boys there that night. He had his family, Georgia, and me. I was like the extra son. I was so happy to be able to go. I wouldn't have missed that for the world. I'm so glad he's in the Hall of Fame, because he's one of us. When I say *us*, I mean the local radio announcers, even though he did television all those years. He's not like the glamorous network guy who gets right in. Al has fought so hard to help the guys who do it every day. To me, it was a great victory for all the local announcers when Al got into the Hall. When someone like Al says something or makes a suggestion, we know that they'll listen. He's the mouthpiece for the rest of us.

---

*A McDonalds now sits where basketball was invented at a YMCA in Springfield, Massachusetts.

HEAR ME NOW
LISTEN TO ME LATER

Greg Schulte

Greg Schulte is the radio voice of Major League Baseball's Arizona Diamond-backs. Schulte joined the Diamondbacks for their inaugural season 1998 and is under contract through the 2011 season. Schulte also covered the Phoenix Suns for many years, where he first produced the broadcasts, and later served as a color commentator to Al McCoy. He also was the original pre-game and post-game host for Arizona Cardinals broadcasts. He is also known by his nickname, "the Governor."

When I came to Phoenix in 1979, I hooked up with Al. I was making the rounds, trying to talk to everybody in the sports business. The major sports in town then were Arizona State University and the Suns. Al was doing the Suns at the time. I discovered that Al and I had a Hawkeye connection when I found out he was from Iowa. I was from the Quad Cities and had just broken off from doing University of Iowa basketball games when Lute Olson was coaching there. Al and I hit it off right off the bat and became very good friends.

A few years later, the guy who had been engineering for Al on Suns broadcasts quit, and Al immediately asked me to do it. We struck up a long relationship—one that has lasted until today. It's usually a phone call a week—about the family, the Suns, the Diamondbacks, and broadcasting. Normally it's a half-hour conversation. It's been a lot of fun over the years, and I really treasure being around Al.

I believe Al's first love was baseball. When he first came to Phoenix, he was to do the Phoenix Giants AAA baseball broadcasts. He was offered the job as the San Francisco Giants' play-by-play guy twice and he actually did one game for the Giants. He had a great passion for baseball and was a big Cubs fan. He always talked about Bert Wilson and **JACK BRICKHOUSE*** as two of his favorite guys. Al even did some Diamondbacks baseball with us the first year or so. He did some fill-in work, doing some radio and TV.

When Al is doing a broadcast, he stays with the ball game. He realizes, as a lot of younger broadcasters these days don't, that the game comes first. Al is the voice of the team, and he promotes them, but he doesn't get involved with an "I/Me" attitude you hear and see a lot in this business now. I'm not saying that attitude's right or wrong; it's just the way everything has changed. Radio play-by-play is a dying art right now—I really believe that. If you stay focused on the ball game, you respect the game you are broadcasting and you respect the audience. Don't talk down to them. Don't sound like you know everything. You can make mistakes. For those reasons, Al has always been one of the best broadcasters that I've ever heard.

I had a chance to go to his Hall of Fame induction a couple of years ago. It was great. I had to miss three of the Diamondback games because we were still playing. My wife Nancy and I went. Al had us sitting at the head table with Georgia and his boys and their families, along with Joe Proski and his wife, Jan. I was honored to be at the head table with him. That was quite a thrill.

Al was humbled by the whole experience. I had talked to him about three months earlier and said, "Al, what do we have to do or who do we have to call—what's the story?—to get you into the

---

***For many seasons, JACK BRICKHOUSE was the TV announcer for both the Cubs and the White Sox. The teams would televise home games only. The first voice heard when WGN-TV went on the air in 1948 was that of Jack Brickhouse.**

Hall of Fame?" He said, "I have no idea what they do." Then, a little less than three months later, I was on a road trip, and he called me. He said, "I wanted to let you know. I just got a call from Springfield, Massachusetts, and I'm going into the Hall of Fame." After his family, I was the first one he called. I got goose bumps.

Al is a straightforward guy. I remember in 1989, we were doing a Suns preseason game in **OHIO***. I was the engineer, and another guy was doing color with Al. I get on the bus and go to the gymnasium. I didn't see Al, so I thought he'd be coming over later. At about an hour before the game was scheduled to start, there was still no Al. I go into Cotton's office and said, "I'd better tape the pregame show now because Al's not here yet." I do the show, but afterward Cotton said, "You'd better give Al a call." I called him at the hotel. He had fallen asleep! He had set his alarm, but we had switched time zones so many times on that trip that the clock wasn't right. That's probably the only time that's ever happened to Al. He rushed over to the gym and got there about 20 minutes before game time. Al was so upset with himself and was totally flustered. But, when the light went on, he was sharp as a tack. There are always little distractions going on behind the scenes that the audience doesn't realize. When you go on the air, you can't give any hint that something was wrong. Al was really embarrassed about that, but he came through like a pro.

Al is the consummate professional in doing his job. One thing he's always talked about is how much it means to him when he receives either a phone call or a letter from someone who is visually impaired, praising him for the way he describes the ball game—pinpointing exactly what is happening during the broadcast so they can almost "see" the action on the court. They are so

*In 1976, Indiana, coached by Lee Corso, scored early to lead Ohio State 7-6. Corso called a time-out and had his team pose for a picture in front of the scoreboard. That picture was on the cover of the Indiana's 1977 recruiting brochure. Ohio State won the game 47-7.

grateful to have a broadcaster who is so descriptive in his call of the game. Those are special things that always mean so much to him.

...how much it means to him when he receives a phone call from someone who is visually impaired, praising him for the way he describes the ball game—

When you listen to Al do a broadcast, he'll have a little fun here and there, but 99 percent of the time the game is going to take care of itself, and your job as a broadcaster is to report it and be as accurate in your description as you possibly can. That's the difference, to me, nowadays in the play-by-play guy. That's why I like radio so much better than television. That's probably the reason Al went to radio also.

On television, you have a producer and a director, and they want to go into different areas. You see that in our telecast, where our guys go. They're showing people in the stands. I can understand when you are struggling, and in some ball games you have to do that. But when the team is playing well, stay with the action of the ball game itself. Get to the other stuff when you really need it.

I always wanted to be a baseball broadcaster. I had a pretty good relationship with Jerry Colangelo and was doing ball games with Al at the time. When the Diamondbacks arrived, Al said, "I know you love baseball. You've got to talk to Jerry. I'm going to talk to Jerry, too; it's a great opportunity for you. You ought to give it a chance." I wanted to do it, but I didn't know if I would even be considered. Both Al and Joe Gilmartin put in a lot of good words for me and went to bat for me big time.

It's been a thrill for me to be able to do Diamondbacks baseball. I always stop and think how very few people have had the opportunity to broadcast a major sport. I treasure it every day. I look forward to every game. Every time I go into a season, I think about Al, and I listen to him during the basketball season just to remind myself how to broadcast a sporting event. You give the game the utmost respect. Al so respects the game itself and the players who play it. That comes out in his broadcasts. These athletes are so good, but they still do some staggering things that are unbelievable, and that excitement comes out in Al.

One thing that's tough for Al is working with an analyst. In basketball especially, it's so hard to work an analyst into the broadcast because the action is so fast. He and Tim Kempton have a really nice rapport with each other. The one thing Al always told me about color commentary is that "you have to be quick with your comment because I have to get back to the action." That's respect for the listening audience. The people want to hear what's going on, so if the ball crosses center court, I'd toss it back to him. He works well with his analyst in probably the toughest sport to broadcast.

Al McCoy, to me, is a really good person—a Midwesterner who made it big. But you'd never know he was a professional broadcaster, or a Hall of Famer, because of his humble demeanor. Al wakes up every morning excited about going to the arena, wherever that arena is. To be honest with you, I don't see him slowing down any time soon. He might tell you it's a "wait and see" attitude for him right now. But I still think he has the desire, the passion, and the love of the game to continue indefinitely.

I can't stress how much he's meant to me in my broadcast career—probably more than anybody I've ever met on the broadcast level. I always remind myself—stay with the ball game, stay with the ball game—as Al does. You can't go wrong doing it that way. He's a great person, friend, and mentor. We talk once, twice, maybe four times a month on the phone. We have a great relationship, both professionally and as friends.

My father passed away two years before I did my first Diamondbacks broadcast. He would have been going nuts about that. Al has been a guy who I've always turned to if I had a question—any question. I hate saying he's a "fatherlike" figure, but maybe he's an "older brother" who I can talk to about anything.

One year, Al and I were doing a Suns game at the Coliseum. I'm the engineer, and he's got Cotton working with him. As we wrapped up the broadcast, Al's voice started to give out. He called me after the game and said, "I'll tell you what. We're going on a trip tomorrow up to Seattle. Be prepared for a phone call because my voice isn't there." Al had never missed a ball game. I got up that morning, and he calls and tells me to get to the airport. "I'll meet you there. I'm going, too, but you may have to do the game for me." The next morning, I get on the plane and fly with the ball club up to Seattle.

Lo and behold, the next day, Al had a mild case of laryngitis and didn't have a voice, so I had to broadcast the ball game that night with Cotton. I'd done Iowa games and Al felt fine with me doing the game, but I leaned on Cotton a lot that night. I was the first person ever to sit in for Al on a broadcast, and I was nervous as heck. Here I was, sitting in for the legend, Al McCoy!

He's a fixture down in Phoenix. Any time you get a room named after you, you're doing okay. He's got a room named after him down at the arena's media center. He's got a booth with his name on it at Donovan's, which is the best steakhouse in the Valley. He's a great Hawkeye, a great announcer, a great guy.

Chapter 6

PUT ME IN COACH

Short Coaches & Tall Players

It's hard to say anything bad about Joe Proski because "The Prosk" was everyone's main man. In his more than 30 years with the Suns, he was the trainer, the equipment manager, the strength and conditioning coach, and the traveling secretary all rolled into one. He did a terrific job. Joe was the type of guy where, whatever you needed, he was there. If it was changing a seat on the plane, making sure you got your per diem, or taking care of your luggage, he was the main man. Joe became one of my best friends through the years and, of course, he still is.

Paul Silas had a great career as an NBA player, and part of that was in a Phoenix Suns uniform. He was involved in one of the most controversial trades in the early days of the Suns. Silas was a real leader on the Suns in the early years but was traded to Boston for Charlie Scott. In that deal, Silas became the "player to be named later." Years later, Silas came back to Phoenix as a member of the Suns' coaching staff. Paul is a tremendous individual, was a rock-solid player, and, later, a dependable NBA coach. On Suns road trips, he was always the target of a lot of kidding because he was constantly nibbling out of a big jar of peanut butter! He was always trying to keep his weight down, and I guess he did it with peanut butter! We'd look over, and there was Paul with his spoon eating his peanut butter. Maybe he had a new system for diet and weight control. I don't know!

In the early years, Connie Hawkins probably did more than any other individual to make the NBA a success in Arizona. He came from a controversial background, as a lot of folks know. If you haven't read his book, *Foul!*, you certainly should. He had an unbelievably difficult childhood and a remarkable early basketball career. He was banned by the NBA for ridiculous gambling allegations that had no basis in fact. He played for the Globetrotters and then went on to dominate the early years of the American Basketball Association. Eventually he was cleared to play in the NBA, but his best years in basketball may have been behind him. He was a vital piece for a young Suns franchise because he was such a great player and had a lot of charisma. The fans loved him! He was great with youngsters, and with his huge hands, he could do absolutely anything with a basketball. Years later, "Dr. J," Julius Erving, said frankly that his whole game was predicated on watching Connie Hawkins and picking up moves from the Hawk!

When the Boeing 747 first came into service, I had a lot of fun with Hawk because those original planes had a lounge with a piano keyboard. I looked at Connie Hawkins' hands and figured out he could probably reach two octaves on that keyboard. On some of the longer trips back east, I'd get Hawk up there in the lounge and try to teach him a few easy pieces on the piano. I can't remember if he ever got through "Chopsticks" or not!

If you want to have fun anytime, on or off the court, call Leapin' Lamar Green. He's a great golfer, who often returns to Phoenix to win a lot of tournaments. He's a guy with a great personality, who always had a smile on his face. And man, could he sky! That's why we called him Leapin' Lamar!

Neal Walk is a terrific guy and probably one of the few true centers the Suns ever had. Prior to the 1969 NBA draft, the Suns and Milwaukee Bucks, the two newest teams in the NBA, were salivating to draft 7'2" Lew Alcindor of UCLA, the top college prospect in the nation. But the Suns lost the coin flip to Milwaukee, and the Bucks got Alcindor. The Suns then picked Walk, who had been a solid All-American at Florida. Neal had some great years with the Suns. Following his playing days, surgery on a spinal-cord tumor put Neal in a wheelchair, but he remains indomitable in spirit and is still part of the Suns' organization.

Garfield Heard is best known in basketball circles for his "shot heard around the world" that sent that amazing Game 5 at Boston Garden in June of 1976 into its third remarkable overtime period. Heard played collegiately at Oklahoma for Suns coach John MacLeod and was obtained from Buffalo midway through the 1975–76 season in a deal for John Shumate. Heard and Curtis Perry teamed up to form a tremendous tandem on that Suns front line. Heard was a consistent contributor that year and every season he played throughout an outstanding NBA career. He's also coached in the NBA and divides his time now between Atlanta and Phoenix.

Back when Jerry Colangelo had taken the coaching reigns in the early 1970s, we were on a Midwest road trip. Jerry was looking for someone to come in and coach the Suns. From his playing days in the Big Ten, Jerry had some kind of relationship with **BOBBY KNIGHT***. All of a sudden Bobby Knight turns up on our team bus on a couple of occasions. Through the rumor mill, we heard that there was a strong possibility that Bobby Knight was a candidate to become the new coach of the Suns. Obviously, it didn't happen, but I am quite sure there was protracted discussion between Colangelo and Bobby Knight at that time. Knight would have lasted about two weeks in the NBA. You simply can't coach players in the NBA the same way you have the hammer over them in college. That's the bottom line.

*Texas Tech's basketball arena, the United Spirit Center in Lubbock, is on Indiana Avenue. Texas Tech's nickname is the Red Raiders. The nickname of **BOB KNIGHT**'s Orrville, Ohio high school was the Red Raiders....In the 1962 NCAA semi-final—Ohio State versus Wake Forest—Billy Packer of Wake Forest had 17 points while Knight failed to score. It was Knight's last college game, as he did not play in the title game. ...

Alvan Adams was another player from that 1970s era that was recruited and played for John MacLeod when he was the coach at Oklahoma University. Adams was the Suns' first-round draft pick in 1975 and immediately became an instant contributor to the team. In his first NBA season, he was named Rookie of the Year, was named to the All-Star team, and helped the Suns to their first NBA Finals appearance.

There are lots of stories about Alvan Adams and his voracious appetite! When training camp started during his rookie year, the whole team went out to the Pine Cone Inn in Prescott for dinner. They would set up a section of the restaurant for the players, and I always went to the dinner. I'd talk to the players about dealing with the press, and I happened to wind up sitting with Alvan Adams. They came around to hand out the meal, and Alvan had the shrimp cocktail. Then he had a nice big salad. Then he had a steak and lobster dinner with a sour-cream-and-chives baked potato. They came around for dessert, and he had apple pie with ice cream. The servers were doing a great job. They were probably impressed by the players. After everyone finished, they asked Alvan if they could get him anything else. He said, "Yeah! I'll have a shrimp cocktail and a salad, a steak, and lobster..." He did the whole thing all over again!

But Alvan was a tremendous player, a subtle individual, and an astute person. He now is in charge of the entire US Airways Center complex. Every time I see him, I think he could still play! He hasn't gained a pound since his playing days.

Ronnie Lee was a guy who came into the league out of Oregon that everybody loved. From day one, he was Mr. Hustle. The Suns marketing department came up with the "Ronnie Lee Floor Score Contest" that kept score of how many times Ronnie hit the floor during a game. That's the type of player he was. Half the time he was on the floor diving for loose basketballs or trying to poke it away from the opposition. He was a very popular player. He did not have a very long NBA career due to a knee injury and wound up playing in Europe for a number of years following that. But Suns fans from the early days will always remember Ronnie Lee and his Floor Score Contest.

Paul Westphal was a student of the game, both as a player and as a coach. He did so many amazing things throughout his career. A trade with the Celtics, perhaps, one of the best moves the Suns ever made. They gave up a great player in Dennis Johnson, but in Westphal, they got a young player who had been languishing on the Boston bench. Paul became an immediate hit in Phoenix. He could score the basketball and do just about anything in a basketball game that you would want. You may remember that in that triple overtime in Boston Garden, with one second left on the clock, he was the one that called a timeout when the Suns didn't have any, giving a free throw to Boston. But that meant the Suns got the ball back at center court, not the baseline. The move set the stage for Gar Heard's dramatic shot that tied the game and sent it to a third overtime.

He was unconventional. He would go to a practice and might wind up in a shooting contest with a player or up in the stands trying to shoot the basketball from there. He has a great love for the game, and it's great to see him back in coaching. He's now in Sacramento.

Johnny High's life, of course, had a tragic ending in a car accident, but in 1979 the Suns had a young guard tying to make the team named Hosea Champine (pronounced like the beverage *champagne*). He never made the club, and I don't know what happened to him, but in a preseason game, I had the opportunity to say something I'd been waiting to say since early in training camp. A loose ball was knocked away on the defensive end and Hosea picked it up and threw it to High, who went in to score, and I got to say, "High from Champine!"

Ira Terrell, out of SMU, had a very short career with the Suns, but I really loved him because I had a great line for him when he scored! "I.T. for two!" Tea for two!

Truck Robinson came to the Suns in a midseason trade from New Orleans. Prior to the deal, I remember sitting in coach MacLeod's office with a few of the owners. One of the owners said, "What do you need to make this team better?" MacLeod responded, "We need a player like Truck Robinson." The trade was made. He came in and was a strong rebounder, a good defender, and had some nice years with the Suns. I'd have to rate Truck Robinson as one of the best-dressed players ever to wear a Suns uniform. He never left the locker room on the road without a suit and tie. You had to like that! I'm so happy that he is now back in the NBA as an assistant coach to Paul Westphal in Sacramento. He's quite a golfer and was very close to being on the Senior Tour.

Dennis Johnson, "DJ," played at Pepperdine collegiately but earned a spot in the NBA with his defensive play. He was a great defender. While he was with the Suns, he was named to the NBA's All-Defensive team, and he gave you that competitive edge every night. He had great years with the Suns, Sonics, and Boston Celtics. DJ passed away just a couple of years ago. It was a tragic loss of a young life.

"The Cookie Monster," Jeff Cook, was one of those players who always gave you just as much as he possibly could every night. He is a great family man and has remained here in Phoenix since his playing days and will always be remembered as a Phoenix

Sun. The Cookie Monster! He's now a hard-working insurance man here in the Valley.

Larry Nance was a very popular player because of his enormous leaping ability. He was a shot blocker and, of course, won the NBA's first slam dunk contest! When the Suns traded him to Cleveland, the fans knew they would miss him, and they did. He went on to have an unbelievable career with the Cleveland Cavaliers. Leaping Larry Nance!

The slam dunk contest has frankly worn out its welcome. It's strictly fan oriented. Most of the great slam dunk players don't want to be involved in it anymore. The league has a tough time getting players to compete.

Al Bianchi was an assistant coach to John MacLeod in the NBA Finals series with Boston in 1976. Following a 10-year NBA career as a player, he was a head coach in both the ABA and NBA. He was with the Seattle Sonics and later went on to become general manager of the Knicks. Basketball has been his life since his college and pro days. One of his best friends in the NBA was his old Syracuse Nationals teammate, the great Johnny Kerr.

I used to say that we had one guy on our team who was willing to fight. The only problem was, it was our assistant coach, Al Bianchi. I'll never forget when we were playing Houston, and Moses Malone was in his heyday. Moses had been fouled, and it was a very controversial call. It put Moses up on the free throw line. As he stood there, waiting to put up his free throw, there was a great hush in the crowd and you could clearly hear the voice of Al Bianchi saying, "Your mama sure named you right! Moses!" Al has thrown a few clipboards in his time, but he was very competitive in his playing days and maybe even more competitive in coaching. He has been scouting around the NBA, but right now he's retired and living in Phoenix.

Jeff Hornacek was drafted in the second-round by the Suns out of Iowa State. Being from that area, I had followed his career, but I was not a Cyclone fan growing up having gone to Drake and the University of Iowa. Once Hornacek came to the Suns, he had a lot of his game altered. Jerry Colangelo likes to take credit for the fact he saw the way Hornacek shot the basketball and worked with him to change it until he became an outstanding NBA shooter. When he was traded to Philadelphia as part of the Charles Barkley deal, a lot of people really hated to see him go because Jeff was a really tremendous person and player. We felt sad because he was a Midwest guy, who came out west and then was banished to Philadelphia. The good news for Jeff is that he didn't stay there very long because he was traded to Utah and went on to have an unbelievable career under Coach Jerry Sloan and the Jazz. Now retired, he makes his home in Phoenix.

Do we have a former player who has gone into politics? Yes we do... Kevin Johnson, or "KJ." In fact, when he was enshrined in the Suns Ring of Honor, KJ didn't think he would ever go into politics. But he did and is now the mayor of Sacramento, his home town. We all know what a great player KJ was! In fact, people forget that at one time, the Suns had Kevin Johnson, Jason Kidd, and Steve Nash on their roster at once. That's three pretty fair country point guards. But Kevin Johnson was one of the best. I can't forget his driving determination and the abuse he took physically. He would take the ball to the hoop and get knocked down. He would have 25 assists in a game. No question about it, he was a competitive, winning player.

But the thing I'll always remember about KJ is that he grew up in Sacramento and not on the good side of town. But he made up his mind that he was going to make the place he grew up a better place to live, and he did that. He started St. Hope Academy, which is an academy to help youngsters with their school work. He then purchased his old high school, Sacramento High School, when it was going to be closed. He turned it into a very successful charter school. He's also built shopping centers in his home area and has done a tremendous job. As a result, as mayor of Sacramento, he is getting a lot of national play for the job that he has done. All of us who know KJ are very proud of him, not only as a person but also for what he's been able to accomplish on and off the basketball court.

Mark West came in the same trade that brought Kevin Johnson to Phoenix. A seven-footer, Mark was a solid NBA center. He did what was required. He defended, blocked shots, rebounded, and set picks. He didn't score a lot. Cotton Fitzsimmons used to laugh and say, "You know you're going to get the ball the first two or three times when the game starts, but after that, you're not going to get it at all." Mark, of course, was a terrific guy, a finance major at Old Dominion who went on to become a stockbroker. He is now involved with Phoenix as an assistant general manager. Mark West is still a team player and a big contributor to the Suns organization.

Eddie Johnson had an outstanding career in the NBA and had a close relationship with coach Cotton Fitzsimmons. When he was with the Suns, he won the NBA's Sixth Man Award and was a great clutch shooter and a big-time scorer. I'll always remember the night that the Suns traded Eddie. We were playing the New Jersey Nets and Cotton Fitzsimmons was our coach. When

I came down to catch the bus over to the arena, I noticed Cotton was huddling with some of the other team officials. I couldn't figure out what was going on. When I got to the arena, I was trying to find Cotton to do my usual pregame interview with him. He was always so open and so available, but on this night, I looked all over that arena but couldn't find him.

Finally, I corner Cotton and he said, "You're going to have to duck in here with me." He was in a little room with Eddie Johnson. I sat down, and Cotton tells Eddie he's been traded. Eddie can't believe it because he was all dressed, ready to play the game. Cotton says, "We'll talk more, but we're going to try to get you a flight out of here tonight, so get dressed." He walks out and I'm sitting there with Eddie. He picks up the phone to try to call his wife and breaks down in tears because, obviously, he loved Phoenix and had this relationship with Cotton. He knows that's part of the business and he went on to finish up a great NBA career. That was a very emotional moment for him and for me. Here I am sitting in the same room when Cotton has to tell Eddie he's traded. Eddie, of course, now makes his home in Phoenix with his family and he is an analyst on the telecast. He worked with me for a number of years and is just a great guy and family man.

Tom Chambers came into the NBA with the Clippers and then spent a few years with Seattle. When a new NBA collective bargaining agreement went into effect, he became the league's first unrestricted free agent and signed with the Suns just prior to the 1988–89 season. To me, Tom Chambers was one of the best-scoring big forwards to ever play in this league. He had an unbelievably quick first step to the basket and, believe me, he could score the basketball! In 1990, he had an amazing 60-point game at the old Coliseum. He was responsible for some big wins when he was with the Phoenix Suns. He's still involved with the team as an analyst on pregame, halftime, and postgame shows. He's also involved in real estate and development.

Cotton Fitzsimmons was the director of player personnel when the Suns drafted "Thunder" Dan Majerle in 1988. We had a big draft party for our fans over at the Convention Center, but when the Suns made the pick, it was booed. Cotton didn't scold people very often, but he scolded that whole crowd that day. He said, "You're going to regret the fact that you ever booed this young man!" He was right. Dan Majerle eventually became one of the most popular players ever to wear a Phoenix Suns uniform. He knew only one way to play the game and that was all out. He was known for his drives to the basket, and he developed his three-point shooting. When the Suns had the inside-outside game going in the Barkley days, Dan Majerle became one of the top three- point shooters in all of the NBA.

He was a very emotional player. That's why everybody loved him. His middle name was "Toughness." He would not back down from anyone at anytime. I'll never forget a game- winning shot that he hit at the America West Arena after which he jumped up on the press table and right into the crowd to show how excited he was about winning. Winning was Dan Majerle.

We couldn't believe when he was traded to Cleveland. We were in Flagstaff at preseason training camp, and it was announced that he was being traded to Cleveland for John Williams. That day, I walked back from practice with Dan. I was shocked at the trade, and Dan was in tears. He did not want to leave Phoenix and could not believe that they would trade him. I couldn't either. He went to Cleveland for a while and then wound up being a great contributor in Miami, where **PAT RILEY*** just loved him. It was great that Dan was able to come back and finish his career in a Phoenix Suns uniform, where he belonged. Then he

*It is true that NBA Coach **PAT RILEY** never played college football, but was drafted by the Dallas Cowboys. His brother, Lee, played seven years in the NFL. It is not true that Pat Riley combs his hair with a pork chop.

Williams School

1950

Dorothy Trampel, *sec.*

Harold Walker, *pres.*

L. B. Shelton, *supt.*

Dick Knickerbocker, *v. pres.*

Leona Minard, *treas.*

Marlys Barz

Charles Walker

Richard Hoefer

Patricia Hames

Albert Vibholm

John Knosby

Allen McCoy

Gordon Bentley

Ann Ruby

Betty Arends

Duane Jansen

With Raymond Burr, better known as "Perry Mason".

MEN OF MUSIC

EXCITING

KRUX 1360

MUSIC
AL McCOY
m. to 12 noon

MUSIC
DICK GRAY
n to 4:00 p.m.

FOLLOW THE

PHOENIX GIANTS

PLAY-BY-PLAY

ON

KOOL - 960

ALL HOME AND AWAY GAMES

WITH

AL McCOY

Al McCoy

Voice of the Phoenix Giants

ALSO LISTEN TO KOOL RADIO FOR
EXCLUSIVE PLAY-BY-PLAY OF
SAN FRANCISCO GIANTS BASEBALL

EXCLUSIVE SUN DEVIL RADIO COVERAGE

ESE TWO VETERAN SPORTS REPORTER

THE VOICE OF THE PHOENIX SUNS!

Al McCoy

If you want to see the Suns on radio, just listen to **Al McCoy!** McCoy's the kind of play-by-play announcer who puts the game right in your livingroom.

And Dick Van Arsdale brings you the color only the former Suns star can give.

From pre-game interviews to post-game "Suns Talk," travel the nation with KTAR 620 – and get a winning game!

And whether you want to know scores or make predictions, KTAR's Sports Team is ready.

THE SPORTS VOICE OF THE SOUTHWEST!

| Lee Hamilton | Tom Dillon | Greg Schulte |

Arizona's #1 Sports Talk host delivers great interviews with a wide field of sports newsmakers and stars.

Weeknights from 6 to 10, Arizona's sports fans listen to "620 Sportsline."

"The Voice of A.S.U." has been voted "Arizona's Best Radio Sportscaster" for a few years running – and with good reason. Dillon brings you the personality of NCAA Sports like you've never heard it before!

Schulte knows sports inside and out – and his in-depth interviews with players and coaches add perspective to the scores.

If you can't be at the games, be listening!

KTAR 620

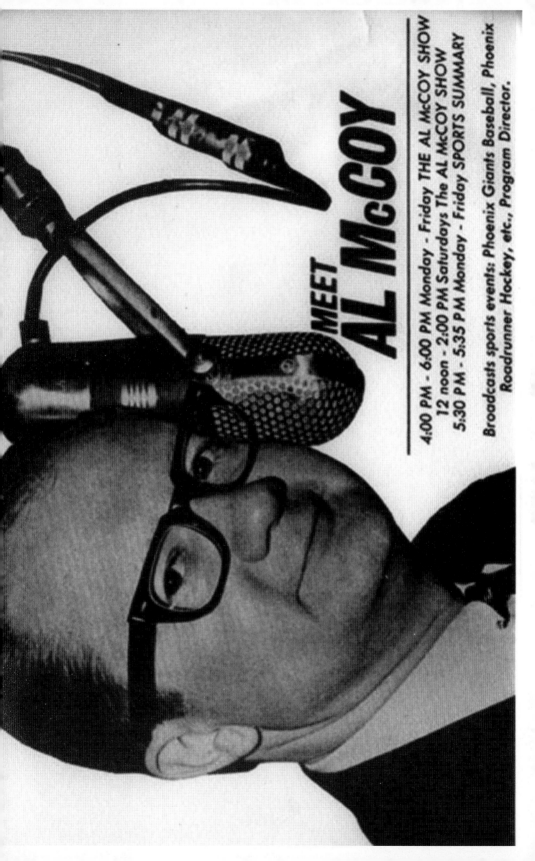

MEET AL McCOY

4:00 PM - 6:00 PM Monday - Friday THE AL McCOY SHOW
12 noon - 2:00 PM Saturdays The AL McCOY SHOW
5:30 PM - 5:35 PM Monday - Friday SPORTS SUMMARY

Broadcasts sports events: Phoenix Giants Baseball, Phoenix Roadrunner Hockey, etc., Program Director.

The ASU Connection: Walter Cronkite,
Al McCoy and Al Michaels

Al with legendary Hot Rod Hundley

Al McCoy Trio with Lamar Green (left)
and Connie Hawkins (right)

Dick Van Arsdale presenting 1000 Game Trophy

Cotton and JoAnn Fitzsimmons
Joe Proski and Al McCoy

Two NBA Legends: Al McCoy of the Phoenix Suns
and Chick Hearn of the Los Angeles Lakers

With close friend Cotton Fitzsimmons

Al with the Big Boss, Jerry Colangelo

Two Valley Favorites:
Charles Barkley and Al McCoy

L MCCOY

Upper Deck Trading Card

Game Time: Eddie Johnson and Al McCoy

Some day, modern technology will invent a bobblehead that actually looks like the real person.

Al McCoy

Georgia and Al McCoy

Mr. and Mrs. Eddie Lynch, Jerry Colangelo, Bill Heywood, and Mary Morrison

Jerry and Mike McCoy (Al's sons), Bob Cousy, Al McCoy

Mr. and Mrs. Greg Schulte

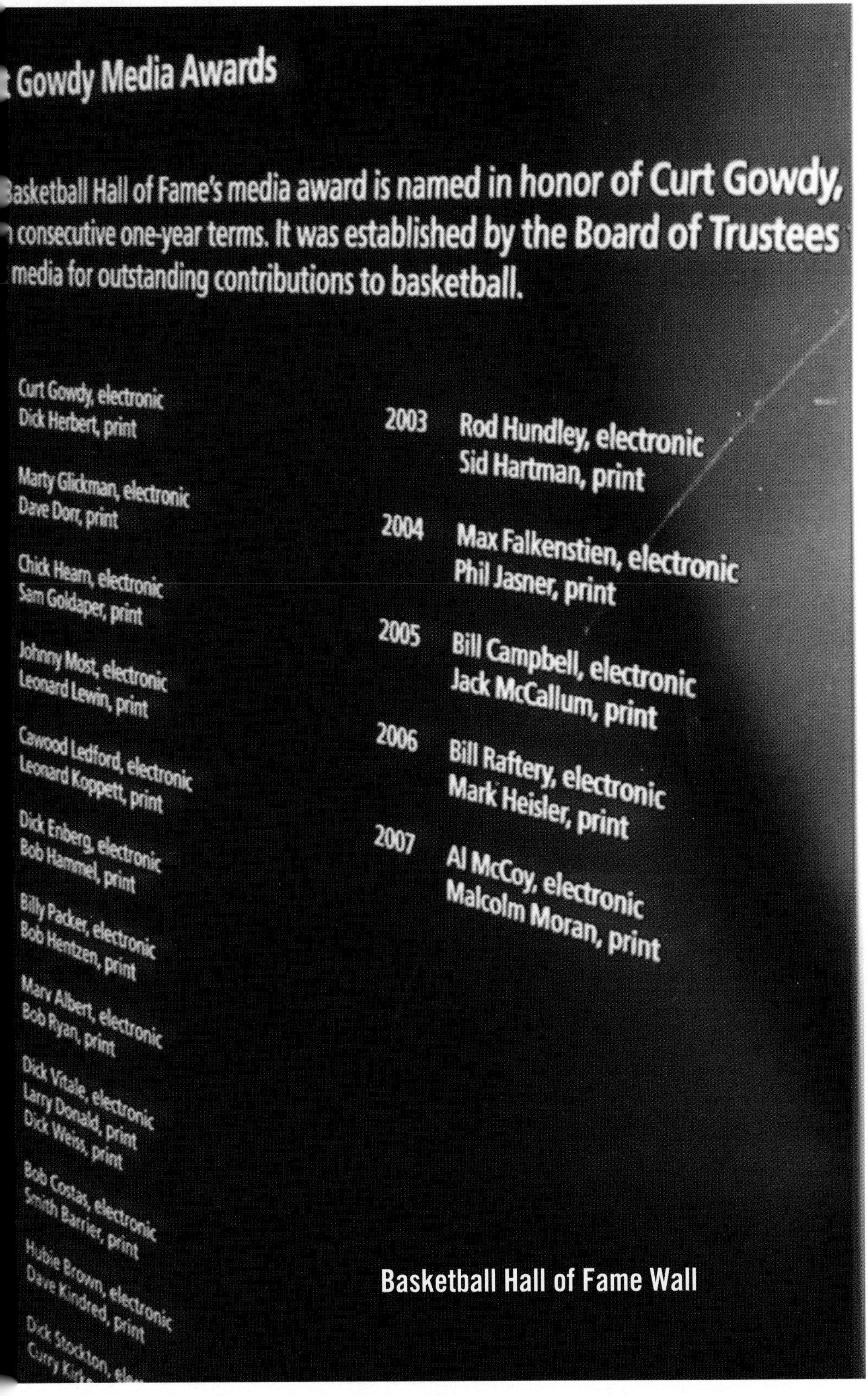

Gowdy Media Awards

Basketball Hall of Fame's media award is named in honor of Curt Gowdy,
consecutive one-year terms. It was established by the Board of Trustees
media for outstanding contributions to basketball.

Curt Gowdy, electronic
Dick Herbert, print

Marty Glickman, electronic
Dave Dorr, print

Chick Hearn, electronic
Sam Goldaper, print

Johnny Most, electronic
Leonard Lewin, print

Cawood Ledford, electronic
Leonard Koppett, print

Dick Enberg, electronic
Bob Hammel, print

Billy Packer, electronic
Bob Hentzen, print

Marv Albert, electronic
Bob Ryan, print

Dick Vitale, electronic
Larry Donald, print
Dick Weiss, print

Bob Costas, electronic
Smith Barrier, print

Hubie Brown, electronic
Dave Kindred, print

Dick Stockton, electronic
Curry Kirk...

2003	Rod Hundley, electronic Sid Hartman, print
2004	Max Falkenstien, electronic Phil Jasner, print
2005	Bill Campbell, electronic Jack McCallum, print
2006	Bill Raftery, electronic Mark Heisler, print
2007	Al McCoy, electronic Malcolm Moran, print

Basketball Hall of Fame Wall

The McCoy Family at the Hall of Fame Induction

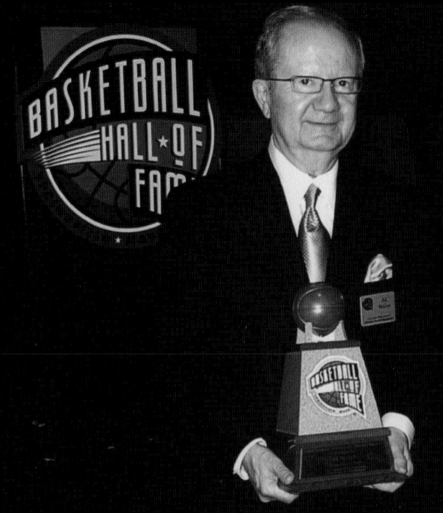

Basketball Hall of Fame Reception, 2007

For Tom
with best
wishes for
every thing
"Good"

Hoop

worked with the team on television and now is a member of the Suns' coaching staff. Dan Majerle is going to become a successful coach in this league.

Greg Grant was a guy I really liked. He was a little mighty mite at about 5'7" and had a one-year stint with the Suns in 1989–90. Why did I like him? I could wear his warm-ups! We called him "Go-Go" Greg Grant.

Cedric Ceballos' claim to fame is that he won the NBA's slam dunk contest blindfolded! How 'bout that? You go into the record book for that! Ced was a guy that loved to score the basketball. He would come off the bench firing. We called him the "point-a-minute-man" because his points scored usually matched his minutes played, which is a pretty impressive stat. He was a key contributor to the Suns' success in the 1990s and now is an important part of our game night crew as the on-the-floor host at all of our home games. But he'll always be remembered for that blindfolded win in the slam dunk contest.

It's hard for me to talk about Wayman Tisdale. He's the player that always had a smile on his face. A big-body forward, he came off the Oklahoma University campus as a great college player, spent part of his career with the Phoenix Suns, and was a contributor. He was also one of the nicest guys you'd ever want to meet. We had a lot in common when it came to music. He loved music and guitar! On road trips, he always took his guitar. When he retired as a player, he started his own jazz group, and they had a number of top-selling CDs. At one time, Wayman Tisdale's group had a CD that was number one in the jazz world.

But Wayman had health problems, and cancer eventually claimed his legs. When the 2009 NBA All-Star Game was in Phoenix, the NBA Alumni Players had a big luncheon, and Wayman was there. He got to see so many of his friends and former team-mates. Everybody wanted to talk to Wayman and encourage him in his battle back. In spite of his problems, he was just as happy and personable as ever. He told us how he loved his family and how good God was to him, and he had that smile on his face. Unfortunately, a few months later, we lost Wayman Tisdale. When you lose an individual like Wayman Tisdale, there is a tremendous void.

Shawn Marion, "the Matrix," was a very popular player with the Suns. He came to Phoenix from UNLV and proved to be a quick jumper and an active scorer. He could run the floor, score, and was a defender that could guard any position in the game. During his time in Phoenix, he was one of the franchise's most popular players. Was there controversy when he was traded for Shaquille O'Neal? No question about it! Shawn's agent was feeding him information suggesting that the Suns didn't appreciate him enough. But Marion was already the highest-paid player on the Suns team at that time. I don't want to diminish in any way the many contributions he made to the Phoenix Suns over his nine strong seasons here. Shawn was a great individual and an exciting player both offensively and defensively. Since he was traded to Miami, he has since gone to Toronto and is now a member of the Dallas Mavericks. We wish him only the best, and Shawn will always be loved in Phoenix.

What can you say about Amaré Stoudemire, except perhaps that his future is still ahead of him. Amaré made the jump from high school into the NBA and was an instant success. A tremendous offensive talent, he has improved his game every single year he has been in the league. But his injuries have been a problem. Knee and eye surgeries have hampered him. He's a hard-working individual and feels he can come back and have a great year. Those of us who know Amaré feel he certainly has those capabilities. He does a lot for the community and charitable causes. He just made a big contribution to his home area down in Florida for a program benefiting underprivileged kids. Amaré Stoudemire is a tremendous individual talent, but the best is yet to come.

Vinny Del Negro was a smart 6'4" guard who had a nice college career at North Carolina State, played in the NBA, and also played in Italy. He was right at home in Italy. Believe me! He played portions of two seasons for the Suns toward the end of his career. After his playing career was over, he found a seat next to me on our Suns radio broadcast. He had a great passion for the game, and although he liked working the broadcasts with me, he really wanted to get into player personnel and front-office work. He did that for a time, but I knew he always wanted to coach. It wasn't a surprise to me when he was named head coach of the Chicago Bulls. That's where he is right now, and he has a great career ahead of him. I am so proud of Vinny.

Jim Fox was another one of the Suns' big men. He came off the campus of South Carolina and joined the Suns in the franchise's second year. He was a very strong inside player and rebounder, could score the basketball, and was a good passer. Jim Fox, his boys, and his wife still live here in the Valley, and we see him at a lot of games.

Frank Johnson was another popular guy while he played with the Suns. He had the ability to come off the bench in the fourth quarter and get things turned around. As a result, he was known as "Fourth-Quarter Frank" for a long time. He played collegiately for Wake Forest. He played for the Suns for just a couple of years, but he eventually came back and became the head coach of the Suns for one full season and portions of two others. But Fourth-Quarter Frank, as we know and love him, still makes his home here in the Valley of the Sun.

Rich Kelley was another seven-footer who played for the Suns. He played collegiately for Stanford and came over in a deal with New Jersey. He spent several years in a Suns uniform. I remember when Rich got here; he was an unconventional guy but a super individual. He was looking for a car. When you're seven feet tall, it's a little hard to find something to fit into. He ran across an old convertible. I can't remember the model, but he took the front seat out and drove the car from the back seat. He was quite an attraction around town driving that convertible from the back seat. Rich still makes his home up in the Bay area.

Maurice Lucas had quite an NBA career, and the Suns made him part of their history when they made a trade with the N.Y. Knicks in 1982, sending Truck Robinson to the Knicks for "Luke." Luke had the perfect size for a power forward, about 6'9" and 235 pounds. He played collegiately at Marquette, but in the pros he quickly established a reputation as an enforcer. He loved to mix it up and never backed away from anyone out there on the floor or anyplace else.

I remember one road trip to Dallas with Luke. In the bar of our hotel in Dallas, there was a piano player. It was a sunken piano, where they had seats all around the grand piano for patrons. Before we left for the game we noticed that there was a gal in there playing the piano. Maurice Lucas always thought he was a great singer, and he knew I played piano. We talked about going back to hear this gal play after the game.

After the game, Maurice, Joe Proski, and I went back to the hotel and went in to take our seats. Again, I want to emphasize that the seats were sunken beneath the ground floor but equidistant to the piano. The gal that was playing the piano was just getting ready to quit for the night, and there were only a few people in the bar. Maurice said to the piano player, "Al here plays piano; could he play?" She said, "Sure, I'm just finishing up but go ahead and sit in and play!" She left, and I come around and start playing the piano, and Maurice is singing "That's What I Like About the South," or something like that.

Now here comes a hotel security guy. This security guy has his uniform on, and he has all the weapons—the gun, the billy club—but he's only about 5'8," pretty solidly built, but a little overweight. He comes storming up and says "Cut this out! You're not supposed to be playing the piano! We have to stop this right now!" Maurice turns around and, again, because we're in a sunken pit, Maurice is looking at this guy's knees. Maurice says, "Well, we checked, and the gal playing the piano said it was OK." The guy says, "I'm telling you it's not OK, and I want it stopped right now!" Well, just then, Maurice, all 6'9" of him, starts to get up, and the more he got up, the bigger he looked and the smaller the security guy looked. Finally, Maurice just went down, grabbed him by the lapel, and pulled him up, eye to eye. "They told us my man could play the piano," he said, "and we're going to play the piano. Goodnight." The guy turned around and walked out.

Cotton Fitzsimmons and I had a great friendship. Our backgrounds are very similar. He was from a small town in Missouri, went to a small high school and college, loved sports and people, and coached on every level. When he coached at Moberly Junior College, he used to bring his team up to play the Drake freshmen. Then he went on to be an assistant coach at K-State and ultimately their head coach before Jerry Colangelo gave him a shot to come into the NBA with the Phoenix Suns.

When Cotton and I first met, I was still broadcasting Roadrunners hockey. Cotton said many times that when he saw me with the Roadrunners he said, "We've got to get this guy." Even before I joined the Suns, we recognized that we had a lot in common... people we both knew from the Midwest, growing up in small towns, and our love of music. Cotton loved Sinatra, big band, and jazz. When he left the Suns and went to Atlanta, he invited us over to his house the first time the Suns traveled there. As the years went by, the friendship continued. Even when Cotton was coaching in other cities, we'd always get together after the game when the Suns played there. When he came back to the Suns a few years later, the friendship just continued to mature.

In the last six years of his life, we really spent a lot of time together and had many great conversations. We talked about growing up and things that were important to us. We talked about good times and bad. We were very, very close. What a shock it was when he passed away. Cotton and I had just finished up broadcasting the Suns season. He had been having trouble with a little hacking cough. I was giving him lozenges and trying to get him cleared up, but he was still complaining about it. When the season ended, he said he was going into Good Sam to get checked because he thought he had bronchitis. I was going there as well for some routine blood work. I was there when Cotton and his wife walked in, and we were joking around. When my blood work was done, I took off. Later in the afternoon I gave Cotton a call, but I couldn't reach him. I called his wife's cell phone and got her. I said, "JoAnn, where's Cotton? What's going on?" She said, "We're in the hospital. They admitted Cotton, and it's not good news. They did a chest X-ray and they found some cancer." Cotton never smoked.

In spite of the diagnosis, Cotton was just as positive as ever. He was in the hospital starting chemotherapy, and he had everyone smiling. I talked to him a little while later and asked him if he was having a tough time. His response was just, "Oh! I'm going to get this thing beat...no problem!" One night I called him, and he said, "Well! I'm putting the top down on the car! JoAnn and I are going for a drive!" All I could say was, "OK, have a good time! I'll talk to you tomorrow!"

He came home that night and went to bed. The next morning JoAnne got up early and had been up for a while but hadn't heard anything from Cotton. She walked in the bedroom and realized he had suffered a stroke. He was never able to speak after that, but he lived for several more weeks. When he had visitors, you could tell that he knew you were there. He'd hold your hand and give you a squeeze, and he knew what you were saying. During his last week, Cotton was at home and a Catholic priest, who was a good friend of the family, was at that house 24 hours a day. The stream of visitors was nonstop. It seemed like every player who ever played for Cotton came by. Each player would come to the house, go in and sit on the bed, and talk to Cotton for a few minutes. It was unbelievable!

Big Rick Robey came to the Suns by way of the Celtics and, before that, **KENTUCKY***. The Suns got him in the Dennis Johnson trade, because they needed a big man. Because of injuries, Rick never really played a lot for the Suns; 61 games in one season, four in the next, and 46 in his last season. In spite of all the injuries, he was a fun-loving guy! On the road, we just loved having him around. He loved people from Kentucky. You might be in a bar or restaurant after a game and someone would say that there was a table of people over there from Kentucky, or some Kentucky fans, and he would pick up their whole tab. He was just that kind of a guy. We had a lot of good times. He and his wife spent some New Years Eves with us. He didn't have the chance to contribute much as a player since injuries consumed most of his time. He departed the Suns when his contract expired in 1986.

Alvin Scott was a collegiate player at Oral Roberts University. Alvin came into the league as a late-round draft pick, and the strongest part of his game was his leaping ability. He could sky, no question about it. He was the type of player that just gave you

*In the 1970s, *<u>KENTUCKY</u> basketball recruited 6-foot 10-inch Parade All-American Bret Bearup from Long Island. After a high school game, Bearup was approached by an up-and-coming coach who said, "Hi Bret. I'm Jim Valvano, Iona College." Bearup looked down and said, "You look awfully young to own a college." Bearup is now the top honcho at the Denver Nuggets.

everything he had every night. It's hard to imagine that Alvin Scott was a seventh-round draft pick in 1977. He spent eight years in a Suns uniform and still lives here in the Valley of the Sun. We see him quite often.

John Wetzel was first drafted by the Lakers out of Virginia Tech but went into the service and was taken by the Suns in the 1968 expansion draft. He didn't come back to play for Phoenix until he got out of the service in 1970. He was with the Suns for several years as a player and eventually went on to become an assistant coach under John MacLeod and ultimately the head coach of the Suns. But my story about Wetz goes back to his playing days when I had the pleasure of introducing him to the famous buffalo chicken wings at Frank and Theresa's Anchor Bar in Buffalo, N.Y. He never forgot it. He loved his chicken wings. He's retired from his longtime coaching days and has a home down in the Tucson area now and one in Hawaii. But whenever he gets to Phoenix, he gives me a call and says, "Let's have chicken wings!" We have a joint here in Phoenix, Nino's, that is run by relatives of Frank and Theresa's, and that's where Wetz likes to go for his wings.

Dick Snyder was another early Suns product. He had played at Davidson and was taken in the expansion draft. He played 81 games in his first year, scored in double figures, and had a very nice floor game. Early in his second year, he was traded to Seattle. Dick has continued to make his home here in the Valley and has a very successful insurance business. His wife, Terie, was a school teacher here for a long time so the Snyders are a very vital part of the Phoenix community. I see him at a lot of games. He follows the Suns, no question about that!

Georgi Glouchkov, the first NBA player from the Eastern bloc countries, was taken by the Suns. He spoke very little English. He's the only player ever on a post-game show I had to have an interpreter.

Georgi Glouchkov, the *Balkan Banger*. Unfortunately, his career was just one year, and he went back to Bulgaria, but it was interesting having him around. He had a pet drink—vodka, coke, no ice.

You probably have to go back to Charles Barkley or Tom Chambers to find the greatest individual game by a Suns player. Tom once scored 60 points in a game. Going back to the 1992–'93 playoffs, Charles made some remarkable contributions. His series against San Antonio and hitting the winning hoop against Golden State both come to mind. You'd have to say he's been involved in some of the biggest wins in the Suns' history.

Through the years of the franchise there have been so many great wins that it's hard to pinpoint one game as "the best." There's never a bad win or a good loss, but because the Suns lost that 1976 triple overtime game in Boston Garden, the triple overtime Suns win in Chicago Stadium in 1993 became more significant. The Suns won that NBA Finals game, and that was a tremendous confidence builder in that series. That would certainly have to be considered one of the great wins in the history of the Suns.

I'd have to go back to Walter Davis for the best shooter in Suns history, although we've had some great ones. Rex Chapman was a great shooter. Of course, Dan Majerle. Steve Nash, certainly in modern times, fits into that category. There have been a lot of them, but it would be hard to beat the shooting ability of Walter Davis, "the Man with the Velvet Touch."

As far as best rebounding, I'd pick Neal Walk. When he came out of Florida as the second pick in the 1969 draft, he put up rebounding numbers that still stand in the Suns' record book. Right there with him is Paul Silas. Other good rebounders that come to mind are Truck Robinson, Charles Barkley, Curtis Perry and Gar Heard.

When you talk about the front office of the Suns, you have to talk about Ruthie Dryjanski. Ruthie had been with the Chicago Bulls working with Jerry Colangelo, Joe Proski, and Johnny Kerr.

When that group moved to Phoenix, Ruth joined the exodus from Chicago. For Jerry Colangelo, she was more than a secretary and assistant. She has stayed with Jerry all the way and was one of the loyal, dedicated Phoenix Suns employees. If you needed something done, needed to see someone, or needed an answer to almost any question, Ruthie would be there to get it done for you. She is a wonderful lady and had a terrific career with the Suns. She's just a great person. She retired at the same time Jerry did.

> **Creating a Suns All-Time Team is too tough.**

Creating a Suns All-Time Team is too tough. I've been asked that question so many times, and it's just too hard. You'd have to do it by eras. The first eight to 10 years of the Suns, it's Dick Van Arsdale, Connie Hawkins, etc. Then you move into the Walter Davis era. Then, it's Paul Westphal, Kevin Johnson, Barkley, Stoudemire and Nash. It's just too difficult to pick five players since the beginning of the Suns to put on that All-Time Team. There have been too many good players.

There have been so many terrific players who have worn Suns uniforms; it would take several more books to give my thoughts on them all. I think they've all been great! The current Suns team certainly falls into that category also. But I do have to mention two veterans, Steve Nash and Grant Hill.

What can you add to what has already been said about Steve Nash? He's won two NBA MVPs...and has been a sensational player and an even greater person. And what a privilege it has been to have Grant Hill with the Suns. No one enjoys playing the game more than Grant and, oh brother! ...how he plays it! Steve and Grant are as impressive to me off the court as on the court. They are both winners in the game of life!

Everything wasn't always rosy concerning the Suns and their long history in Phoenix. Certainly one of the times that was particularly upsetting to everybody was in the late eighties. There had been lots of talk about drug use in professional sports. Unfortunately, the Phoenix area had a county attorney and a chief of police who were looking to make a high-profile drug case against persons of notoriety. We found out later that they had keyed in on the Phoenix Suns.

We discovered that they had people following Phoenix Suns players. Even after a practice session, if a player stopped at a coffee shop for breakfast, they'd have every car in the area checked out by motor vehicles to see if any known drug dealers were there. They even started to think about perhaps gambling going on. I thought it was a witch hunt at the time, and my mind has never changed.

There were multiple indictments and lots of news conferences and sensationalized media coverage. **HOWARD COSELL***, an attorney as well as a writer and broadcaster, found what was going on in Phoenix quite interesting. He did a column in the *New York Daily News* that spells out the circumstances better than I can. We received permission to reprint this article, and I think it tells a great deal of the story.

Howard Cosell
New York Daily News
May 17, 1987

Their names have been printed in papers across the nation. Their faces have appeared on television sets across the country. Reputations have been maligned by rumor, hearsay, innuendo, and by secret grand jury testimony leaked to the media.

*When former ESPN and current NFL Channel anchor Rich Eisen was in college, his stand-up comedy routine included reading "Letters to Penthouse" using HOWARD COSELL's voice....John Lennon's death was first reported to the nation by Howard Cosell on Monday Night Football...

Their guilt has been proclaimed everywhere but in a court of law, by a jury of their peers. Is this the way of America?

The men are basketball players. Three of them—James Edwards, Jay Humphries, and Grant Gondrezick of the Phoenix Suns—were indicted by a Maricopa County, Ariz, grand jury for "conspiracy to possess cocaine," "conspiracy to transfer cocaine," and "conspiracy to transfer marijuana." Two former players were also named, plus Walter Davis, who was not indicted and who is in a drug rehab center again for treatment. Along with these indictments and "namings" also came reports of a gambling scandal centering on the Suns and the Milwaukee Bucks.

Now, most recently, hearsay grand-jury testimony was leaked to the media in which the names of Jack Sikma and Paul Mokeski of the Milwaukee Bucks have been implicated in the gambling scandal, and Dennis Johnson, now of the Celtics and formerly of the Suns, has been named as a cocaine user. Johnson denies the charge. And Johnny High, the former Sun who said Johnson used coke in 1982–1983, now retracts his statement. To date, no one has been indicted in the gambling scandal, and no indictments against Sikma, Mokeski and Johnson have been issued.

But transcripts—I repeat, transcripts—of the grand-jury testimony have been published, huge segments of it in *The Arizona Republic* and *Mesa-Tempe Tribune*, making it possible for any newspaper or television station to pick it up and use it.

Grand jury testimony is meant to be secret, precisely because it is always full of rumor, hearsay, and unsubstantiated charges. Secrecy is mandated and necessary to conduct investigations to determine if charges can be brought against someone. Anyone can go to a grand jury and say anything he wishes, level charges, and accuse falsely.

It is the jury's job to determine truth and to indict or refuse to indict for lack of evidence. That is the American way.

But no longer. This reporter has watched in horror the contempt for the judicial system and for constitutional protections exhibited by the Maricopa County Attorney's Office and the media. These two groups face a grave crisis, and they had better do some very deep self-examination concerning their roles as law-enforcement officials and as the purveyors of information and champions of the people's right to know.

Let's begin with Tom Collins, the county attorney, and with James Keppel, the deputy county attorney in charge of the Suns' investigation. I spoke at length with Keppel. Keppel may mean well. He may be speaking the truth when he says he is deeply concerned about the leaks and is trying to stop them.

But when this reporter asked if the leaks came from his office, he said, "I deny that." When asked why no other indictments have been issued when so many names have been made public, he had no comment. He had no comment when asked if he realized the potential damage done to men who are to be presumed innocent until proven guilty.

He had no comment, whether the question was about his responsibility to the law or if Sikma, Mokeski, and Johnson, too, are to be indicted. Keppel was full of concern, but vastly unwilling to express any real indication of that concern.

Keppel and his superior, Collins, could take a lesson from federal prosecutor Rudolph Giuliani and his staff. They don't leak. They know they are protecting something far more important, even, than any individual's reputation, important as reputation is.

They are protecting American justice. They are protecting you and me in case someone, one day, mentions your name or mine in a grand jury investigation, and you and I have committed no crime, broken no law, taken no drugs, offered no money to players to dump games. That is the American way.

Thanks to the press, this reporter has now read huge chunks of the secret testimony. I have no business reading it, and nor do you, but there it was. As an attorney, I was aghast at the lack of evidence against these men. To echo the *Mesa-Tempe Tribune* editorial of May 10, there are no times, no dates, no places, no quantities.

These specifics may yet be in unreleased police reports, but they certainly aren't in the testimony I read. But to judge from the leaks and subsequent media reports indicting these men, you'd think the grand jury itself actually witnessed all of them gambling or using cocaine.

Is this the way America wants the law and the media to function?

This goes far beyond the innocence or guilt of a handful of current or former basketball players. This strikes at the gut of our way of life. We cannot permit this to continue. I have no personal knowledge regarding these men. I assume they are innocent, because that, too, is the American way, until such time as they are proven otherwise in court.

But I am reminded of a terrible time in our history when I saw things like this happen. I am reminded of Sen. Joe McCarthy and his witch hunts of the late '40s and early '50s. Many of you are too young, or were not yet born, when he held his Senate hearings. He destroyed people's lives, and their reputations, with gossip and hearsay, innuendo and rumor, false accusations, and guilt by association.

That is not America's way. But we let it happen. It took years before he was stopped and finally censured by the Senate. And it was a lone television reporter, the late

Edward R. Murrow, who stood up on TV and challenged McCarthy. And that was the beginning of McCarthy's end.

So, in the Murrow vein, this reporter stands up and challenges the Maricopa County Attorney's office—and law enforcement offices everywhere—to plugs leaks and shut its mouth. And I challenge members of the media to rethink and reconsider before they rush to print or broadcast information that does not further truth, or justice, or give the American people information they need to judge public policy.

Otherwise, we have desecration of truth, justice, and law in the name of scoops and political and reportorial self-aggrandizement.

Let the grand jury finish its work in private. Let the indictments—if there are more to come—be handed down. Let the courts take care of this. Let the jury render its verdict. And above all, let us remember the danger inherent in the situation involving the Phoenix Suns, the Milwaukee Bucks, the county attorney and the media.

McCarthyism was not the American way. But it happened here.

IF LIFE WERE FAIR
THERE WOULD BE NO WHEELCHAIRS

Neal Walk

Coming out of the University of Florida, Walk was the Suns first-round pick in the 1969 NBA College Draft and the number two selection overall. At Florida, Neal was a two-time All-America and was the only major college player in the country to rank among the top 10 in both scoring and rebounding. As a junior, he led the nation in rebounding with 19.8 per game. He played five years with the Suns and parts of three other seasons for the New Orleans Jazz and the New York Knicks. Neal averaged 12.6 points and 9.4 rebounds for his eight year NBA career. His best year in the pros came in 1972-73 when he averaged 20.4 points and 12.4 rebounds as the Suns center. He is also the only Suns center to ever take down more than 1,000 rebounds in a season. He has been confined to a wheelchair since undergoing surgery for the removal of a tumor on his spinal cord in 1987.

Al McCoy's a fun guy. Everything was different when I was a young player. I don't know what the players do on the road today, but we had a little group, Joe Proski, Dick Van, and me. I was a young player, and Al wasn't much older. He knew all the great jazz and blues joints in Chicago or New York or wherever we went. He had recommendations of places to eat. He also has a great sense of humor.

He is a great piano player. Back in the days when we took planes, the 747 had a lounge in the bubble on top, and there was a piano in many of them. Once the seatbelt sign went off, we'd go up there, and Al would start to play. The guys would be drinking beer or wine, and Al would be playing tunes. Sometimes other passengers would make requests, and he would usually know the songs. He was a pretty accomplished musician as far as I could tell. Amazingly, his hands are pretty small compared to ours, but that didn't seem to cause him any problems.

What I knew about Phoenix before I came here in '69 was that it was in the Southwest. I knew the team was an expansion team. I knew it was going to be hot. I came twice—once in May, and it was beautiful. But when I got out of the plane at the end of June, I was standing on the top of the steps in my suit looking down. In those days, you exited the plane and came down the steps to the ground, not into the terminal like it is today. By the time I hit the ground, my jacket and tie were off, my shirt was unbuttoned, and my sleeves were rolled up. When they opened the back door, the air was dry—the dry, dry heat. I'd never experienced that. I thought that if there *is* a hell, this has surely got to be the gateway.

Once we got off the plane in Buffalo, in the same fashion, only in the winter, I was on the top step, and Al had just gotten off the last step, stepping into the snow. Of course, there was always snow there. I yelled down, "Al, how deep is that snow?" He yells back up at me, "Neal, for you, it's going to be about ankle deep, but for me, it's damn near knee high."

Al didn't join the Suns until 1972. No knock on his predecessor, Joe McConnell, but Al was just a different guy. Joe wasn't necessarily an annoying fellow, but with A-1 Beer as a big sponsor, you could be at the free throw line and hear Joe say, "Free throw on its way, Goooood! Like A-1 Beer!" He'd say that every time. By the way, that was a horses_ _ _ beer, but we drank it. You got past the first one, and you were good to go. I was young then, so I tried to stay out of the way of problems.

I love Al's kids—Jerry and Jay—they're great guys. Georgia is a sweet woman—always has been. Al wouldn't knock guys. He never tried to bring anybody down. He'd report the game. He could be critical but wouldn't rip into guys, especially our own. The best thing about Al McCoy is his wide range of stories.

Not too many years ago he told me how, after Joe left, he had nobody to hang with on the road. He missed the old days. Every now and then, we'd try to get some of the guys from those days together, and Al was among them. He's among the best story-tellers I've ever been around. He's got a crack memory, too. He remembers some things from when I was playing here that I can barely recall.

Just becoming a professional basketball player and getting to play against people I'd watched as a kid—people like Chamber-lain, Robertson, and West—made me feel very fortunate. I tell people that I didn't call heads or tails; I just came when they asked, and if they were unhappy, that was too bad. Coming to Phoenix was a real gift. Playing for Jerry Colangelo was too.

I was with the Suns as a player for five years and have been back with them for 20 years working with the archives—digital scrap-booking and images. That's half my adult life. It's pretty cool. I like photography. I don't shoot the images; I just play with them, save them, and print them.

Al McCoy is one of the nicest guys I've ever met. I've never heard anybody say anything untoward about him. I've always enjoyed him. He's always friendly, and Georgia and his sons as well. They go out of their way to say hello. I'm pleased and honored to know Al as a professional and as a person. There's no doubt about the fine work he's done over the years in many sports on his road to this place. He's as big a part of the Phoenix Suns as the building.

There are a lot of short-timers in the game and a lot more that just go for the theatrics. Al uses his catchwords, but he's got a great voice. He's always been a good interviewer. I always enjoyed it when it was my time to be interviewed right after a game on the floor. That meant I probably had a pretty good game, but it was always fun to go on with Al. He'd laugh with the guys. He was one of us. Now, as we age and times change, he's not like one of the players as much. I don't know what these guys think of him. If they think anything petty of him, they're crazy. He was more like one of us than like management.

Chapter 7

MCCOYPALOOZA

The Wrap-Up Show

IT'S NICE TO BE KNEADED

Joe Proski

Joe Proski was the Suns first trainer, joining the team from Chicago in 1968 and then holding that post for the next 32 years. He was NBA Athletic Trainer of the year in 1987-88 and earned the first 30-year award ever issued by the National Basketball Trainers Association. Joe served as a trainer at four NBA All-Star games. He was named to the Suns Ring of Honor in 2001. His nicknames include "Prosk" and "Magic Fingers."

My wife Jan and I got to know Al's parents pretty well. Longevity is definitely on Al's side. My wife Jan and I drive to Green Bay about three times a year to visit family and friends. We would always stop and see Al's parents in Williams and shoot the breeze with them. His dad was so funny. I think he might have been 95 years old when he passed away. They had lived there on the farm, but when Al's mom passed away, Russell, Al's dad, moved into an assisted living place. Every time we'd visit, I'd meet these people at the little post office downtown and in coffee shops where we'd stop in, and I'd ask, "Hey, have you seen Russell lately?" The lady would say, "Yeah, he was just in today. He stopped at the bank." Even at his age, he was all over town. But eventually they told him he couldn't drive anymore, and man, was he mad! One of the ladies where he lived told us he'd forget where he parked his car. So, Jan and I would go down to his place to see him. It was really a nice place, a lot smaller than the house he'd lived in on the farm. We'd tell him, "Russell, this place is awesome. We think it's really nice." He'd say, "Well, it's nothing to grow old for." We said, "But, it's a nice place, and there are a lot of nice people." He said, "Yeah, but the ladies here are all so old." That was when the guy was almost 95. We always enjoyed going back through Williams.

Of course, he'd always ask us, "How's my boy doing?" A couple of times we were there right after Al had come back for the big Fourth of July parade in Williams where he was the grand marshal.

> He said, "Yeah, but the ladies here are all so old."

Another awesome guy in Al's life, who I got to know, was his coach...coach Lovin. He's a really good guy.

I'm very fortunate. When the Suns went in a different direction, and made changes to the training staff, I thought, "Oh my G--, I'm losing one of my best friends!" I miss being on the road with Al. It was a lot of fun. But we still stay in touch.

For 27 years with the Suns, I did everything myself. Now, they have eight or nine guys on the staff. I'm not saying things haven't changed, but I can't believe things have changed that much.

Al's father, Russell McCoy

CHEVY CHASE ONCE HOSTED THE OSCARS, HENDRIX ONCE OPENED FOR THE MONKEES, JIM ZABEL ONCE RACED JESSE OWENS...THERE ARE SOME THINGS YOU JUST CAN'T MAKE UP!

Jim Zabel

Jim Zabel is a broadcaster best known for serving as the play-by-play announcer for University of Iowa Hawkeyes football games for 49 years on WHO (AM) Radio. Zabel joined WHO as the sports director in 1944, and remains employed by the station as a talk-show host. Zabel broadcast a half-century of sporting events in Iowa, including the Drake Relays. He was named to the Iowa Sports Hall of Fame in 2007. In 1937 Zabel was the Iowa state high school sprint champion and a match race was arranged with Jesse Owens. Guess who won?

Al was a little bit younger than me. He came as a student from Williams, Iowa, a little town about 50 to 60 miles north of Des Moines. WHO is significant because Andy Williams and Roger Williams also got their start at WHO.

Al went to Drake University. He came down here as an announcer, but he was working as a heck of a jazz piano player. He worked Don Hoy's Orchestra. Hoy had a big dance band in the area for a long time. He also played late night gigs. Des Moines was a wide-open town in those days, and they had all-night bars and an all-night entertainment place right around the corner from the station called the Green Parrot. Al would work his shift here at WHO and then go over there and play jazz piano.

He worked as a straight announcer. At that time, I was doing a lot of news and sports. He would fill in for me, and we worked together. He was a young guy, but he had a great voice and was a great jazz piano player. That's what I most remember about him.

I thought he had a definite future. He moved on, and I lost track of him for awhile. Then, I started going down to Scottsdale and ran into him again. Now, we're inseparable. We talk at least once a week. He comes back to Des Moines. He's very active in Drake University stuff. We talk all the time and get together as often as we can when he's in town.

He does a heck of a job down in Phoenix. We're all the last of a breed. We're the Jack Bucks and Harry Carays of the world, guys who are identified so much with doing one particular thing or covering one particular game or team, like he's been identified with the Phoenix Suns for over 40 years. I've done Iowa Hawkeyes play-by-play for 50 years and have been at WHO 65 years. You become part of the team, actually. The broadcast of the Suns wouldn't be complete without the play-by-play of Al McCoy—and I've heard many people say that. He's an inimitable figure down there in Arizona right now.

Al did baseball and some football. He did a lot of different stuff. I know he did the Giants one time down there. He covered a local baseball team. Then, all of a sudden, he made connections with Jerry Colangelo when he brought the team down there, and they hired Al—that was something like 38 years ago. He's been there ever since.

He's in the Hall of Fame, and he deserves to be. He's a great guy and a great credit to the broadcasting business. He's got that fabulous voice, and I always tune him in on the radio. I watch the game on television, but I listen to Al on the radio. He's that kind of a guy.

ACTUALLY, THERE ARE A LOT OF BUSINESSES LIKE SHOW BUSINESS

Mary Morrison

Mary Morrison is the driving force behind Arizona's 12-year-old House of Broadcasting. It is Arizona's premier radio and television museum, dedicated to preserving and celebrating the history, personalities and paraphernalia of the electronic media.

I wanted to know more about Al McCoy. He was one of the first broadcasters we honored because I thought so highly of him. I said to Al, "People don't know anything else about you. I don't ever read anything about you." He is very humble— the Midwest, Iowa, and all that. How he got this far is amazing. Somebody recognized his talent.

Al was the second honoree for the Arizona Broadcasting Hall of Fame. Our first was Mike Owens. The Buck Owens family owned KNIX radio and other radio stations.

Then I said, "Well, let's see." I wasn't thinking of sports in particular. I was thinking of businesspeople in our community. Then I thought of McCoy, who's very much a gentleman. I've known him for many years. His wife is Armenian, as am I.

I thought to myself, "I love Al McCoy; he'd be so much fun to talk about." Not only do I admire him, but I have to pick someone everyone admires. You can admire someone who has done a lot of good, but you need somebody who is well-known because otherwise you won't sell out the house, and that's not good for anybody.

Al McCoy Roast
The Pointe Hilton Resort
April 17, 1999

Welcome	Bill Heywood, Roastmaster
Roast	Bill Thompson
Roast	Tom Chambers
Roast	Pat McMahon
Roast	Sheriff Joe Arpaio
Presentation	Bill Heywood
Roast	Cotton Fitzsimmons
Roast	Kevin Ray
Roast	Bill Schonely, Portland Trail Blazers
Presentation	Bill Heywood
Roast	Dick Van Arsdale
Roast	Jude LaCava
Roast	Connie Hawkins
Roast	Dave Munsey
Introduction of Al McCoy	Jerry Colangelo
Finale	Al McCoy
Goodbye	Bill Heywood
Special Appearance	The Phoenix Suns Gorilla

CELEBRITY ROAST

Honorary Chair	Jerry Colangelo, Phoenix Suns
Master of Ceremonies	Bill Heywood, NewsRadio 620 KTAR
Title Sponsor	NewsRadio 620 KTAR
Contributor	The Arizona Republic
Roast Producer/Director	Maurie Helle, Helle International Inc.
Invitations and Programs	Rick Garrett, BC Graphics
	Debbie McLaughlin & Debra Stevens, SRO Communications
Videotape Resources	SWANK Audio Visuals
	Bill Denney
	Scott Pfister, Dave Grapentine & Steve Miller, Suns Productions
	First Take Video
	Audio Video Recorders of Arizona, Inc.
Piano	Schroeders Organ and Piano of Arizona, Inc.
Jazz	Timothy's
Illustrator	Ron Lee Thomas, Occams Edge Haircutters
	Credits: Sports Cartoonist for The Arizona Republic; Illustrator for "Shazam" book by Bill Levy; Creator of Original Pastel of Al McCoy portrait and 8x10 Black & White Caricature of Al McCoy

We had some great folks at the 1999 ceremony—Hugh Downs, The Lewis family from Channel 3. All the people I chose really admired Al. It was such a wonderful evening. Jerry Colangelo and the Suns Gorilla were there. We had the Suns dancers, too.

At the end, he did his signature play-by-play call and played the piano. People were astounded. We just had a beautiful evening. The Suns helped me put it together, and everybody went all out for Al.

Al is so warm. He has no ego. People who don't know him can walk up to him, and he'll talk to them. And people recognize him. I went to the Basketball Hall of Fame in Springfield, Massachusetts, about two years ago just to see his induction. I told Al I was so happy to see him honored in the Hall of Fame. He said it was a wonderful evening. For him to even say that—nothing gets to him.

The House of Broadcasting is a radio and television museum that showcases Arizona's broadcasting history and personalities. We have a dynamic broadcast industry. We are preserving it from the beginning for future generations. We have Steve Allen, Al McCoy, and Buck Owens material in there. We have some archives. A photo of the young Al McCoy graces our wall, and we even have a *shazam* tee shirt from Al's special night.

We have old cameras and production equipment there. We don't want any of the stations to throw anything away. We started the museum 13 years ago, and now, at 2,000 square feet, we're out of space. We have a big archival area, and I told Al that when he's ready, I want to put his entire collection there, not just the few things I have. He's still not ready to give it up. What an absolutely incredible man.

Even in 1972, my first year doing the NBA, the radio broadcasters were still located up high in certain arenas. At Madison Square Garden, in New York, initially we were up in the old hockey booth. That was ridiculous. We got no statistics or anything. In L.A., at the Forum, we were also up high. For years, the announcers fought to get down on the floor. A few years later, we did. All the broadcast positions were where they should've been—on the floor. "Why do you want to be on the floor?" a lot of people ask. "I wouldn't think that would be a good place to broadcast a game because you could get blocked out or screened out on plays." That is true, but the big plus is that when you're broadcasting a game on the floor, particularly on radio, you get into the "feel" and the flow of the game. At courtside, you can hear the comments from coaches and players. You also have the opportunity to talk to the coaches and players and do more interviews. You have the opportunity to get clarifications of calls from referees. *The* place to broadcast NBA basketball games is on the floor.

Unfortunately, a few years ago, the league and the owners decided those seats were too costly. They thought they should be sold, and the radio people should be moved. They left television and newspaper people there, which is hard to understand. Anyway, they moved the radio broadcasters up to locations high off the floor. It just makes it tough to broadcast a game. The majority of radio announcers in the NBA really are concerned about it, because sometimes you can't see the whole floor. You can't get clarification on calls from officials. You simply don't get that "feel" of the game. On top of that, quite often you're surrounded by unruly fans, certainly not the best of circumstances.

One of the great lines of the last couple of years came from my good friend, Joe Tait. He's the longtime voice of the Cleveland Cavaliers. The Cavs were playing the Celtics in Boston, and the radio broadcast location there is horrible! You're actually blocked from seeing one corner of the court. When a player is in that corner, shooting a three-point shot, you can't see him. Tait, one of the great NBA broadcasters, was doing the play-by-play in his inimitable style when there was a three-point shot from the corner. He couldn't see the player, so all he could say was, "Well, there's a shot from three point range! It's up! It's good! By a player to be named later!" That was just the way it happened.

It is not an ideal situation but apparently one that those of us doing NBA radio have to live with. Obviously, a lot of announcers feel that when you can't see, it's hard to see personnel changes on the floor or understand a referee's call. The radio guys are all flattered when they hear that people turn down the sound on their televisions and listen to the local radio play-by-play. We certainly don't want to make mistakes on calls just because of where we are sitting. But we just can't see all the action. To get back to a permanent courtside location would be something that we'd all relish.

Joe Proski has been one of my best friends. You spend 30 years on the road with someone like Joe, it's just terrific. The Suns never had a more loyal employee than him. He was a trainer, equipment man, traveling secretary, chaplain—about everything you could think of. Our relationship is very close. I remember well when we were on the road and Joe's father passed away back in Green Bay, Wisconsin. He called me early that morning when he'd just gotten the news. He was concerned about who was going to take care of tickets and who was going to take care of this and that. I said, "Don't worry about it, Joe. We'll get it taken care of." We did, with some help from players and other people.

I can't tell you how many times, when Cotton was the coach, we'd get in bad-weather situations, and it was Joe, Cotton, and me taking care of the bags. I remember one night in Chicago, there was a blizzard, and we were trying to leave. All the players didn't want to be out in that cold and snow, and they were dumping our bags out there. Here's Cotton, Joe, and me trying to get the bags inside. I remember turning to Cotton and saying, "This is the big leagues, Cotton. You are a coach in the NBA, right? You're out here scuffling around handling bags?"

Joe Proski has been recognized as one of the all-time great trainers in the NBA and for me, he's been recognized as a great friend. He was in Chicago with the Bulls with Johnny Kerr, Jerry Colangelo, and Ruthie Dryjanski, who was a secretary in the front office there. They all came to Phoenix to be with the Suns, and that's when I met Joe.

We didn't really become close until I got the job with the Suns. We had a lot of similarities. I had been involved in minor league baseball. Joe, although he spent time with the Cubs, had been in the minor leagues for the majority of his career. There are always stories to tell about the days in minor league baseball. And Joe has a lot of them.

When we traveled on commercial airlines, Joe handled all the tickets, seat assignments, and boarding passes. When we got to our gates at the various airports, he would hand these out. As you can imagine, the players were always complaining, "I don't want to sit in A-24," or "I don't want to sit in B-18." We were in Detroit at the airport one day, and Joe had a real hassle trying to get all the tickets and the boarding passes handed out. We were walking down toward the gate, and guys start complaining. Joe just took the boarding passes and threw them up in the air! He said, "Okay, it's pick-up time. Pick them up, and I don't want to hear anything from you." The players had to scuffle around and find a boarding pass, and we finally got everybody on the plane. Joe was great at his job, and in those days, it wasn't easy when we were traveling on commercial flights. But he was able to get the job done.

The head trainer still has some duties along those lines, making sure the buses are there, etc. Most of the travel arrangements now are made by the club. The Suns have their own travel agency within the US Airways Center. Of course, we now have our own charter planes, making it an entirely different ball game. When I heard we were getting our own plane, I said, "Hey, I like this. I may stay in the league a little bit longer." The last few years, traveling commercial with a sports team was really getting tough.

Remember, NBA players are big guys. You get them in those little, cramped seats, it's difficult.

At one time at the airport, they'd have a seating chart behind them with a bunch of stickers on it. When you got your seat assignment, say 12-B, they'd pick the sticker up, put it on your boarding pass, and you were all set. Now you go to the airport and get your seat assignment, and they say, "The computer is out. We're not going to be able to assign seats for a while." In the old days, maybe it was better. Anyway, everything changed for all sports teams when they got charter flights. It's made the travel a lot easier for everyone.

Proski and I are a couple of Midwest guys. Joe is from Green Bay, Wisconsin, and I'm from Iowa. Again, the fact that he had a lot of years in minor league baseball allowed us to really hit it off. We spent a lot of time together. If we had a night off, we'd go to dinner together. He always took care of me, and I helped him. If he needs something I can help him with, he knows I'll do it. It's that way today.

We've had some flights that were pretty rough. Before we got our own plane, we were on a charter flight to Philadelphia. All of a sudden, as we get up to our cruising altitude, the plane, rather than going in a straight direction, was just floating. We wondered what was going on. They assured us it was not going to affect the flight. Now we start to get closer to Philadelphia and, for some reason, they say we're not going to be able to land. We are in the air, waiting, and finally, we go back to Dayton, Ohio, to land there and refuel. About four or five hours later than we were supposed to arrive in Philadelphia, we did get in. They acknowledged they had some problems with that plane. We weren't too excited to hear that at the time.

We had a flight just a few years ago to Houston. All of a sudden, we hit one of those horrible air pockets and went straight down. There was nothing the pilots could do. They had no warning at all. It was so strong that seat belts even broke. Food trays were up on the ceiling. Eddie Johnson, one of our broadcast analysts, who doesn't like to fly anyway, was having a tough time.

I had just returned to my seat and was buckled in when the drop happened. The next morning when I got up to take a shower, I had black and blue marks down both legs and on my arms. That drop did more damage than you might think.

Talking about travel in the NBA, Rod Hundley, my first color analyst, was a member of the Lakers when they were still in Minneapolis. That was in the early days when they were flying DC-3s. The Lakers were heading out of Minnesota, and a big snowstorm hit them over Iowa. The plane got iced up and was forced to make an emergency landing in a snowy cornfield in Carroll, Iowa. Hot Rod used to tell the story that Elgin Baylor was wrapped up in a blanket on the floor. But the people in Carroll, Iowa, were terrific. They came out and took everyone in. Hot Rod can tell you about that. No surprise—the Iowa folks took care of everybody!

Over the last 10 to 20 years, there has been a remarkable influx of foreign-born players into the NBA. And over that time, there has been a tremendous improvement in these players' skill level. You can give a lot of that credit to NBA coaches and players for going to Europe, holding clinics, and working with their teams. Basketball has become a major sport, for both spectators and athletes, all over the world. We still consider **SOCCER*** to be the number one sport worldwide, but basketball's popularity is unquestioned and is growing rapidly.

The coaches and players in these foreign countries were quick learners. Even going back 10 years, some of these European players were already starting to surpass our home-grown American players in the fundamentals of the game. Why? Well, because in the States our system was allowing players to come out of college early, or even out of high school, to be drafted in the NBA. The young Americans

---

*More U.S. kids today play **SOCCER** than any other organized sport, including youth basketball. Perhaps, the reason so many kids play soccer is so they don't have to watch it.

were not sound fundamentally. The European players, on the other hand, had been playing basketball in developmental leagues since an early age, while being drilled on the fundamentals.

That is what we are continuing to see today. During the season, look at the top 10 scorers and rebounders; you're going to see a number of foreign players. What it boils down to is that these players are just coming into the NBA stronger in the fundamentals and as a result are better shooters, scorers, and defenders. It goes back to the fact that NBA players and coaches, through clinics and coaching, helped improve the game overseas. We certainly see it with the foreign players who prove every day that they can compete at the NBA level.

In 1975, the Suns traded their high-scoring guard Charlie Scott to Boston for a reserve guard named Paul Westphal. Also that year, the Suns drafted a college junior out of Oklahoma. He was a skinny, 6'9" center named Alvan Adams. Westphal and Adams teamed up to give the Suns a dynamic one-two punch that would result in a run to the NBA Finals and a Rookie of the Year Award for Adams. I came up with a nickname for this dynamic duo...it was easy..."Westy and the Oklahoma Kid." Westphal loved games like bridge and backgammon and all sorts of board games. He and Alvan Adams had some classic match-ups over game boards.

Westphal, Adams, and I were in Milwaukee, staying with the team at the Pfister Hotel. The hotel featured an excellent gourmet restaurant. We had an off-night so Westy and Alvan went to the movies. When they came back around 8:30, they wanted to get a good meal so they went down to the restaurant. They didn't have the proper attire, but those restaurants always had jackets you could wear. Well, obviously the restaurant wasn't prepared to fit NBA players because the jacket Alvan wore was up to his elbows, and Paul's was small and tight, but they put them on and sat down. As they looked over the menu they said, "What's this steak tartare? Why don't we try it? We like steak!" The server came over, and they asked him to bring them an order. Neither one of them knew what it was, so in a few minutes, here it comes. They take a look at it...Alvan looks at Paul...Paul looks at Alvan, and finally, Alvan calls the server back. "Listen, could you maybe take this back, make some patties out of it, fry it up for us, and bring it back?"

Then it was on to Buffalo. I had worked in Buffalo for a year and I knew that the famous Buffalo chicken wings were invented at Frank and Theresa's Anchor Bar on Main Street. I told Paul, Alvan, and John Wetzel that we had to get down there and get some wings. You couldn't get them any place else. That night Paul and Alvan, always competitors, were trying to outdo one another on how many wings they could eat. Even though Alvan set some kind of record, he wasn't able to play the next night. He got a little ill!

As a result of that, Paul Westphal then opened a restaurant, Westy's Café 44, and brought two guys out from Buffalo to cook chicken wings! Initially it was just a small roadside chicken wing place, but he later opened up a bigger restaurant. The two young guys that came out from Buffalo were terrific cooks! They even took over the food service for the press room at the Coliseum. We had chicken wings and lots of other excellent food. Those guys were great!

Westphal had a beautiful home up on Seventh Avenue in Phoenix and had all kinds of antiques. That summer, Paul and his wife were going on an extended vacation, and they wanted someone to stay in their house. They were going to be gone about six weeks, so the two guys from Buffalo said they'd be happy to watch the place. Well, the only problem was that when the Westphals returned, the restaurant was closed, and the house was stripped. They never found those guys.

It's difficult to recall my first paid commercial in Phoenix, but I'll bet it goes back to when I was doing Roadrunner hockey. It was Charlie Rossi Ford, a dealership in Scottsdale. Charlie Rossi, who was from Detroit originally, was a terrific hockey fan. I met him while I was doing Roadrunner games, and that started a 14-year relationship doing the radio and television commercials for Charlie Rossi Ford. After I finished with the Roadrunners and started with the Suns, I still continued with Rossi. That was probably the first long-term commercial account I had.

I've always been very cautious and selective in doing commercials. I would never do a commercial that I did not believe in. I have to feel that it is a very strong product or company. I've always had an automobile account.

After my years with Charlie Rossi Ford, I thought I might not pick up an account right away, but I did. I got the Buick dealers of Phoenix. I also then did Childress Buick. Following that, I now have a very lengthy relationship with Sanderson Ford-Lincoln Mercury. I've had great relationships with these people, and they've all been tremendous dealers. I've known the president of Sanderson Ford, David Kimmerle, since my days at KRUX. We finally got together, and I'm very proud of the relationship I have with Sanderson Ford-Sanderson Lincoln Mercury.

There are always things that happen when you're doing commercials, particularly in the automobile business. There are times when you get into a car, and it won't start. That means you have to do it over again. Now, with video tape, it's a little easier to correct some of the things you might not have been able to do earlier.

Truth in advertising is a very big thing. I've always held to that principle to the letter. I will not endorse a product if I haven't used it, whether it's windows in your house or carpet on your floor, a swimming pool, whatever the case may be. If I haven't used that product, I don't feel I can go on radio or TV and endorse it. It's the same way with an automobile. If you're going to be talking about a certain brand of car, you certainly have to drive that car, spend some time with it, to be able to adequately and truthfully describe it to a viewer or listener. Probably my favorite car is the one I'm driving now—a Lincoln MKX.

When we are doing a car commercial, I tell them, "We don't want to be like every other car commercial." That's why, on several occasions, David Kimmerle, who's the president of Sanderson Ford, will be on the commercials with me. They've been in business a long time. They have a tremendous reputation. That's what I want people to be aware of. For example, they're never open on Sunday. That's a big thing with them, and yet they're still the number-one Ford dealer in this region. My belief with commercials is, although you can do all these fancy things, and they can be pretty and nice to look at, that people want believability. That's the type of approach I have always tried to use with the accounts I have had.

I've changed car dealerships. Charlie Rossi Ford is no longer in existence. The dealership was sold, and Charlie Rossi opened a Lincoln-Mercury dealership in Woodland Hills, California. I did his commercials there for a while. Childress Buick is no longer in business here either. A lot has changed.

I'm now doing some work for Sleep America. I've done others through the years. Sleep America is great. I don't do a lot for them, but I am involved with some of their promotions. I also make some personal appearances for the clients I work for. I have had the good fortune of being able to be selective in the commercial products I endorse. I don't want to be on everything that's on radio or TV.

The equipment used in producing commercials is so much more extensive than it was 25 years ago. The things they can do now are absolutely amazing. People in the industry today are very knowledgeable and are able to do so much more electronically in producing television commercials in particular.

There are more commercials than ever. From the starting lineups to the injury reports—you name it; it has a commercial connotation to it. Commercialism is upon us.

Dennis Johnson, a great NBA player, had some good years with the Suns and some great years with the Sonics and Celtics. It seemed like every year "D.J." was all-defense first team. As the story goes, Dennis was up in Seattle while the Suns were there, and he had a misunderstanding with a young lady in a hotel who claimed to the authorities that Dennis pushed her around a little. There was a talk show host then in Phoenix named "Hacksaw" Hamilton, and he felt I wasn't being demonstrative enough in talking about the incident on the air.

One morning I get a phone call from a writer at the *Arizona Republic.* He said, "Did you hear what Hacksaw said about you last night? He was asked by a caller if Al McCoy had said anything about the D.J. incident. Hamilton said that Al McCoy is never going to say anything about that." I said, "Oh, that's interesting! As you know, Jerry Colangelo and I talked about it on his show, and I talked about it on John MacLeod's show!" Both of those programs were on KTAR radio, which ironically, was also Hamilton's station. My response was, "Look, I'm not a talk show host. I do the play-by-play. Do you think that story should have been in the play-by-play? Let me ask you this. Name me a play-by-play announcer that you maybe think is one of the most respected in the country." The reporter stopped for a few minutes and said, "Well, probably Vin Scully of the Dodgers." I said, "OK, a few years ago Steve Garvey was having problems. His wife was having an affair, and it was in the papers. Did you ever hear Vin Scully talk about it?"

"No, I don't think so," he said. "There were rumors about a baseball strike. Did you ever hear Vin Scully talk about it? No. Because Vin said 'I talk about what happens between the lines.' When I'm doing play-by-play, I'm talking about what's going on in the game. Now, do you and Hacksaw Hamilton think I should do something like this:

Now here he comes down the right side and throws it to DJ. DJ, a gal filed charges up there in Seattle the other night, looks inside, he passes it down to Adams...

Is that the way I should do the play-by-play?!"

Dick Van Arsdale had a great career in the NBA, and when he retired as a player, he became my partner on our Suns' broadcast team for the next 15 years. We had a tremendous relationship, no question about it. Now, those games were simulcast on radio and television. I certainly remember the very first game we did together! It was in Portland and Van was a little nervous about his first outing. On the night of the game, we came on with our opening, and I have to tell you that at 6'5" Dick Van is a little taller than yours truly. To make the heights look a little more even on television, Dick leaned against a chair. It wasn't really comfortable for him, but at least we looked a little better on camera. The camera comes on, and we start to do our live "open." Just as we did, I noticed that Dick Van got this tremendous charlie-horse cramp in his thigh. Boy! He tried to move, but he couldn't and was clearly in a lot of pain. I did a quick wrap-up and went to the next commercial break. We left our stand-up position, walked around the press table, and I turned to Van and said, "Listen guy! Now you know the tough part of this business! You have just been having fun bouncing that basketball out there. Now you learn what it's like to really be in a tough situation!"

A lot of the catchphrases you use just happen. Sometimes, one will bounce out from something you're thinking about. They used to refer to a Midwest style of play-by-play sportscasting. What did people mean by that? There were a lot of play-by-play announcers in the Midwest and most were very up-tempo, on top of their games, personality driven, and weren't afraid to have a little fun at the same time. You could put Chick Hearn, Harry Caray, Bert Wilson, Jack Brickhouse, Jack Quinlan, and Bill King all into the same category. Since I grew up in that era, with that same type of understanding, that was my approach to broadcasting sports.

When I started doing play-by-play, I used catchphrases. Particularly with the Suns, things just seemed to pop up. One night, early on with the Suns, we were involved in a very close game. In the closing seconds, the Suns had a chance to win. They trailed by one. A player drove down and had an uncontested layup—but it went around the rim and fell off. I don't know how I thought of it at the time, but I said, "Oh, heartbreak hotel!" What came to mind was hearing that Elvis tune back in my disc jockey days. It was all about a guy who had things going so badly that he was down at the end of Lonely Street at the Heartbreak Hotel. Somehow that was all I could think of —that this guy must have felt like he was lonely down at the Heartbreak Hotel for missing that shot. That became one of my staples.

You realize you have something going when fans start repeating it. Usually you are surprised when that happens, but you have to be careful because you can overdo it. I rarely use Heartbreak Hotel anymore, but people still remember it. I used to go into high school gyms, and the kids would have big banners with *Heartbreak Hotel* written on them.

There have been a lot of others: *swisheroo for two, zing go the strings,* and *Oh, brother.* But the one that has become most recognized is *Shazam!* That came about when the NBA put in the three-point shot. I started thinking about baseball announcers having a home-run call. "It might be...it could be...it is!" Or, "It's going...going...gone!" I thought this shot was going to become the home run of basketball, not knowing then that there might be 25 of them in later-year games. I wanted to come up with something to use when one of the Suns hit a three-pointer, thinking there might be just a few in a game. Having been a 5'7" point guard in high school, I feel the three-point shot is a good thing and wished we'd had it then.

I wondered what would best describe a shot like that. When I was a kid I read the Captain Marvel comic books. The young guy who became Captain Marvel was a radio reporter in the comic strip. When he became Captain Marvel, he said, "Shazam," which was taken from the first letters of Socrates, Hercules, Atlas, Zeus, Apollo, and Mercury. When he said that word, lightning and thunder went off, and all this excitement took place. I got to thinking, "Boy, that just might be what to use for a three-point shot." I started using it, and it caught on all over the country. In fact, a short time after that, CBS, who had the NBA national telecast, brought Brent Musburger to Phoenix to do a game. Brent walked over to me before the game and said, "Hey, can I use *Shazam!* tonight?" I said, "Only if you give me name recognition."

Catchphrases like that make it a little more fun for the viewer or the listener. We have to realize that people aren't necessarily listening or sitting there for the whole two-and-a-half hours, so you have to make it fun for them. That doesn't mean we're not going to describe the game accurately or that we're not going to give the team that's winning the right emphasis, because you have to do that. Fans are too sophisticated these days to do it any other way.

A lot of player nicknames just happen. Take Steve Nash. When the Suns originally drafted him, at the press conference somebody turned to me and said, "What's your nickname going to be for Nash?" Right away I said, "Nash Rambler." After the press conference, Steve came to me and said, "What's a Nash Rambler?" Maybe there are just a few of us who know, but the Nash Rambler was an automobile that moved around pretty quickly.

We've talked about Walter Davis a lot, "the man with the velvet touch." He was as smooth as silk with his shooting. He was also called "Sweet D." Things seem to just come up. Sometimes you'll hear a player refer to another player by a nickname you think might fit in. That's how most of those things come about.

Connie Hawkins tabbed me as "Real" for many years. He never called me by my first name; it was always Real. That has probably been my longest-lasting nickname.

Most announcers have their little pet phrases, particularly for basketball. Local announcers are closer to the team because they're doing all the games and are familiar with their market, the city, and the players. However, I don't think anybody ever takes a phrase somebody else is using and tries to use it.

Some of the greatest responses I have gotten through the years have been from sightless people. If there is one thing that keeps me going back for more, as far as continuing to do the Suns game, it's the response that I get from not only sightless people but people who are shut-ins or in hospitals. They depend on the radio and on me for the Suns broadcasts. A number of years ago, I was a guest on a radio talk show. Just as we were ready to go off, the last call came in from a gentleman who wanted to thank me. He told me,"When you're broadcasting a game, I know where the basketball is, I know what the score is, I know where the shot was taken from. You make me see the game. I guess I can say that because I'm blind." I told him that I could not get a greater compliment than that. It's very fulfilling to know you are providing a service to people who really need it. I'm thrilled to be able to offer that service.

A few years ago, there was a 100-year-old retired lady in Sun City who was a huge Suns fan. She had pretty much lost her sight and had been listening to my games for years. She happened to be interviewed by a sportswriter at the *Arizona Republic*, who wrote about this huge 100-year-old Suns fan. She told him, "Oh, I would love to meet Al McCoy, and I hear he plays the piano." The writer told me about it, and I made a call to the retirement facility she lived in to set up a meeting. Her son, who lived in Texas at the time, found out about it and came too.

My wife and I went out to the retirement community. This lady had no idea what was happening. She came in and sat with me at the piano, and I played songs she knew. We talked about the old songs she remembered. She realized it was me as soon as she heard my voice. I got a wonderful letter from her son afterward telling me, "You just can't imagine what this did to lift her spirits." She has just recently passed away.

It's really fun to have an opportunity to speak to broadcasting students at Arizona State University. I've also had enjoyable times speaking to broadcast students at Drake University, my alma mater, in Des Moines, Iowa. I hear from all kinds of young announcers.

For a couple of years we played a preseason game in Syracuse. Syracuse has a reputation for putting out top-flight play-by-play announcers, and I have gotten tapes from students there. I really enjoy it, and I do listen to them. I try to give an honest critique.

Just recently I met a young Syracuse graduate who was doing some college sports broadcasting in the East. I corresponded with him a few years ago and critiqued some of his tapes. He was down South and came to our game in Charlotte, North Carolina. I had the opportunity to meet him and was impressed. I liked his approach to broadcasting and recommended him for the Utah job when Hot Rod Hundley retired. He didn't get the job, but right after that I was happy to get a call from him telling me he was just named the voice of the University of South Carolina sports, both football and basketball, which is a great opportunity for him. It's always interesting to talk to young men interested in the field and then see those who go out and are successful—that really makes it rewarding....

Broadcasting can be hard work. Getting into the business doesn't happen overnight. A lot of people aren't willing to live in small towns and not make a lot of money in order to get the needed experience. Those who do and work to improve themselves usually wind up doing quite well. I always remember, going back to my first job in broadcasting at KJFJ in Webster City, the general manager, Wayne Hatchett, telling me, "Al, the smart guys in this business are the ones who know where their next job is." I've always had that philosophy. Right now I'm not worrying about it, but, through the years, it's not a bad thing for a young broadcaster to keep in mind. The ones who are successful are the ones who are willing to make sacrifices. A lot of these young guys don't realize that holidays and Sundays are just another day when you're in broadcasting....

Coach John MacLeod and I had a great relationship when he was coaching the Suns. At 14 years, he had the longest tenure of any Suns coach and was their winningest coach ever. He took the Suns to the NBA Finals for the first time in 1976. We used to talk a lot about families and what you relinquish to have a job in the NBA. John had a son and a daughter. I have three boys. You miss a lot of things when they're growing up because you're on the road with your team. People don't realize the sacrifices you have to make if you're going to be in pro sports.

The most difficult sport to officiate has to be basketball. It's almost an impossible job. The game is so fast. In most contact sports—football, hockey, and basketball—officials could almost make calls on every play, but that would destroy the flow of the game. Through the years, I've been good friends with some NBA referees, going back to when I came into the league. Fellows like Mendy Rudolph, Earl Strom, and Jake O'Donnell were all highly respected former referees who did a fantastic job.

For many years the NBA operated with just two officials calling the game. Sometimes I think the game was called better that way. The officials I named were really take-charge guys. They controlled the game and were highly respected by the players and coaches. We had a lot less complaining in those days because the referees wouldn't tolerate it.

There came a point when the league decided to make some changes at the top level of officials management. What transpired is that a lot of the veteran guys, with a lot of experience, decided to retire. We saw a lot of *young* officials come in. They also went to the three-man crew. Since then, I don't think the officials have been respected as much as they should be. Well, who do you blame that on? Mostly, I blame it on the officials themselves. They have to earn their respect and have to be able to control the players and the game.

All you ask of an NBA referee is to be fair. That means you call the game the same at both ends of the floor from the opening tip to the closing buzzer. Officiating NBA basketball is almost an impossible task because of the speed of the game and the size of the players. In general, the officials do a commendable job. I would like to see more control by the officials, however. I'd like to see them eliminate some of the constant complaining by players and coaches. We'll just have to wait and see.

As I said, I do respect the officials, but, on the other hand, if an official makes a bad call, one that is obviously incorrect, and it affects the game, then are the broadcasters supposed to report that? We're there to report what's happening in the game. If that call affects the game, we're obligated to report it. The league and the officials might not like that, but the officials are a part of the game. They're not perfect and we realize that.

On the other side of that coin, very early in my career I learned that listeners don't want to hear you complain on every call, and we certainly try not to do that. I know some listeners probably feel that there is too much made of referee criticism, and as a broadcaster, I certainly try not to overdo it. To be honest with you, I've left that more to my analysts. The majority of my analysts have been former players like Tim Kempton and Vinnie Del Negro, Keith Erickson and, of course, Dick Van Arsdale, so I let them criticize the officials if they feel it's necessary. It's part of the game, anyway you look at it. You have to report the good and the bad.

Traveling and "palming the ball" should be called. That gets back to the consistency of the officiating. And, do certain players get away with certain things? Those of us who have been in the league a long time think that maybe the superstars are handled a bit differently. The age-old question is, "Is this something that comes from the top level of the NBA down to officials?" That obviously would be denied by the league. Again, if a player palms the ball or travels, it should be called.

What we see in the NBA too many times is that at the start of the season the intention is to make all those calls or eliminate complaining, but somehow along the line, it gets pushed to the side. Again, consistency in officiating is the key. All players and teams should be handled the same. Calls should be made at both ends of the floor.

There have been times when an official has been hurt and has not been able to continue. It's not as easy job; there's absolutely no question about it. I have nothing but respect for them and the job they do. Their travel is horrible. They fly commercial; they're jumping on planes day and night.

I've had a philosophy for a while that the league doesn't go along with. I would like to see crews work together for the entire season, as we see in baseball with their umpiring crews. In the NBA, you have a different officiating crew every night. If they put crews together, even if just for half the season, it would make a big difference. You would have a real veteran official, another official who maybe has been in the league five or six years, and then maybe a new official who has been in the league a year or two. You'd have more consistency. These younger officials would only be better because they'd be working with a senior veteran official every night. It would improve officiating in the NBA a great deal. I've been a proponent of it for many years, but the league doesn't seem to feel that it's the way to go.

One thing the league does right is providing very good security for the referees. They come on and off the court with security people. They have their own locker rooms. The security all over the league now is good. Obviously we've had incidents, such as the one in Detroit a few years ago. We don't want to see things like that where the fans get involved with the players. It just can't exist. You can't have it in any sport. Security, unfortunately, will probably be an ongoing problem.

Many times I've seen fans charge down and try to get onto the court, screaming and yelling at officials, but they don't get very far with that anymore because security is right there. We have had some incidents where players have gone into the crowd. Charles Barkley was once accused of spitting on a fan in Philadelphia.

We had an incident in 1976 in Game 7 in Oakland, when Ricky Sobers and Curtis Perry got involved with fans. While a play was going on, a fan came onto the floor and grabbed Curtis Perry. A fight broke out and several Suns and Warriors got involved. Ricky Sobers mixed it up with the Warriors' Rick Barry, but none of Barry's teammates came to his aid. Barry won't agree with this, but that incident seemed to dampen the spirits of the Warriors, even though they were the defending NBA champions at the time. It seemed to shift the momentum, and of course the Suns went on to win the game.

Outside of Phoenix, it's hard to name a favorite arena. What factors in to my decision is whether I am right down on the floor. There aren't many of those anymore. When we play the Lakers in Los Angeles, I'm on the floor, and there's still something special about playing the Lakers. At Chicago, I'm on the floor, and Chicago is one of the best big cities—a great sports town. It's always terrific to be in Chicago. We have a great broadcast location there. They would probably be two of my favorite places right now. The fans in those places are great.

In some of the other cities, the fans can get a little out of whack—whether you're a broadcaster or not. In most cities, the fans are knowledgeable. You get to know them through the years. I used to love it in New York when we were down below because a lot of those fans have been around for years. Now we're up in a terrible location where we don't see anybody except the guy who goes by with the cotton candy.

US Airways Center is the best-kept arena in the NBA. Although it opened in 1992, it's stayed immaculate through the years and has already been remodeled. The new pavilion entryway is terrific. It's right up there with some of the best. The exterior of Dallas' American Airlines Arena is a little bit overwhelming, but it's really a terrific arena. Any time a new arena goes up, it's out-standing, but, as I said, US Airways, because of the way it's been maintained and remodeled, is still rated very high. The Dallas arena is beautiful, both inside and out.

Conseco Fieldhouse in Indianapolis may be the best pure-bas-ketball arena. It was designed like the old fieldhouses used to be. From that standpoint, it's really terrific. The Indiana fans have a great place to watch basketball. Their practice court has win-dows open to the street where the fans can walk by and watch the team practice. It is an ideal place and, from a fan standpoint, is one of the best places to watch a game.

Profanity can be a problem. We've had some situations where a feed came in from an unknown source with someone yelling and using some profanity about the game. That happened at US Airways Center a few years ago. Fortunately, it did not get on the air. Somehow these comments were getting into the system and going out into the arena. Some people thought it was get-ting on the air, but fortunately it wasn't. They were able to track it down to an open mike that had been left behind and was pick-ing up conversation. Engineers have to stay on top of stuff like this. They are generally aware of where they're placing micro-phones now, so they're not left where they're going to be picking up a fan yelling profanity. Security helps with this also. Before every game, an announcement is made to the fans that profan-ity is not going to be tolerated. Usually if there is a fan who starts swearing, there's another fan nearby who calls security, and it's brought to a very quick stop.

I don't think announcers are very much in fear of problems like that now. You see that happen more on national TV, where they have everything miked but the basketball. Just this past season, the national television people wanted to have the coaches wired at halftime. It was supposed to be controlled. They had a person from the NBA in the TV truck monitoring everything before it went out on the air. One of the very first times they tried it, the

Utah Jazz were playing in Phoenix, and Jerry Sloan, one of the greatest coaches ever, was making a point at halftime. He used a profanity, and it was picked up and broadcast nationally on TNT.

I don't feel that coaches, managers, and players from any game should be interviewed during the contest. I guess you could say, "Well, he's old school." Didn't you like it when there was some mystery to the game? Why do you have to know why the coach did this or that or what they're going to do in the next half? Isn't it fun, from a fan standpoint, to make a guess about what their strategy is going to be in the second half? I think it's overdone.

National television is a big dictator of what happens in professional sports. We're all very aware of that. Whether the fans really appreciate or enjoy it, I don't know. I do know this: a lot of coaches I know in the NBA don't give too much information in their short little interviews. It's mostly, "Hi. We're good. We played all right. We'll do better in the second half." What does that accomplish? After the game, it's always good to get a player who has made a big play, and the fans like to hear from that individual. But it's overdone a bit.

Dick Vitale is one of the great guys of the game. What he's done for college basketball, with his TV work, is more than we can even mention. He was briefly a coach in the NBA with the Detroit Pistons. Early in his first year, the Suns went to play Detroit in the bubble, the Silverdome. John MacLeod was our coach. Before the game, I saw Dick Vitale, and he said, "Where's your coach? Where's Johnny?" I said, "Do you mean Coach John MacLeod?" He said, "Yeah, where's Johnny?" Well, no one called Coach MacLeod "Johnny." John was in the media room, so Vitale goes in to visit with him. MacLeod really wants to get back into the locker room to prepare his team for the game, but he's not able to break off the conversation with Vitale. I'm standing off in the wings, and John catches my eye. I know what he wants, so I go up and say, "Coach MacLeod, they want you in the locker room." Gratefully, John walked off toward the locker room.

The game was only four or five minutes old, and there's a call that goes against Detroit. Dick Vitale runs out onto the floor and starts chasing the referee. The referee is trying to get away from him, and they wind up running all around the court, with the referee leading the way, and Dick Vitale on his tail. Coach Vitale was ejected from the game. His NBA coaching career won't take you very long to talk about. But what a great guy and what a great job he's done in promoting college sports.

Two things make a great NBA coach, and maybe the most important is the ability to deal with players. Cotton Fitzsimmons was one of the best. I thought Mike D'Antoni had that attribute as well. I think Alvin Gentry does. But Cotton Fitzsimmons was one of the best because he had the ability to get all the respect he needed from his team. If a player was not playing well, if he was not doing the job defensively, Cotton would get him out of the game and say to him, "You want to play in this game, pal, you better get going, or you're going to be sitting down next to me the rest of the night." Maybe right after that game, Cotton would go up to the guy with his arm around him, "You're my guy, pal, you're my guy. You did it for me." He had the ability to really get on a player when needed, but he was also skilled at being on the good side of a player too.

A coach has to know how his approach to the game and how to use his personnel. You have to play the type of game that matches the personnel you have. Some coaches struggle to adapt to the personnel they have, and they want to play another type of game, but you can only use the personnel you have. You have to be able to make some adjustments.

There was always criticism of the simulcast, mainly by people who didn't know anything about it. A lot of newspaper people were critical of it, saying that the announcers talk too much, etc. But I would put all the years we simulcast Suns' games up against any that were strictly TV. We used replays and did all the things necessary. I used to tell my analysts, "Remember, you don't have to say, 'Well, as you can see now.' You can talk about the play on the replay, just don't say, 'We're going to let you look at this now.'"

The NBA convinced teams to abandon the simulcast, and the Lakers, Suns, and Jazz were the last to give it up. Nobody does it now. There are so many different sources for the games; you have local radio, a Spanish radio station, local TV, and you might have national TV or cable. There are a lot of broadcasting crews....

In pro sports, and probably more so now than ever with all the sports talk shows, there are all kinds of inaccurate rumors put out on the airways on a daily basis. One of them through the years has been the moving of franchises. I don't think it's as common now in sports as it might have been at one time. If a particular city is not drawing well, or if the team's not winning, there's always the rumor about them being on the move or going to be sold. It's not that easy anymore to move a franchise. It's a big job, a big responsibility, and it costs a lot of money.

I don't think the Suns have ever come close to moving. After the late eighties, when that so-called witch hunt with the drug scandal was going on, things were at a low ebb, and there was some thought the team might move. The team was actually sold, and that's when Jerry Colangelo's group purchased the franchise. They've been very solid from that point on.

The Suns had been very successful for the original owners. Slowly, the team had been able to buy out some of the limited partners, all of the Hollywood people who bought in early. The last one to go was Andy Williams, who was much more of a major owner than Tony Curtis, Bobby Gentry, or Ed Ames, who all had limited partnerships.

I've met Andy Williams many times. He's from Wall Lake, Iowa. He's a terrific guy. When he was one of the owners, he and Henry Mancini used to come to the Coliseum to sing the Anthem and perform before the games....

Usually you can smell a coaching change coming on. The tipoff is when they seem to lose contact with the players. When a team isn't winning, it usually leads to all kinds of speculation. You can't fire the whole team, so, unfortunately, it's usually the coach who has to go, whether there's a problem with him or not—many times there isn't. But the coach takes the rap. It's never easy. And it's not easy for the new coach who has to come in at the middle of the season to try to pick up a ball club. Still, coaching changes are prevalent. Look around the NBA at the coaching changes made each year. The same thing prevails with other sports.

John MacLeod was probably the most underrated coach of the Suns. He came relatively early in franchise history, so people today aren't that familiar with him. MacLeod was from Indiana. He coached high school basketball, was an assistant at Oklahoma University, and then became their head coach. He was there six years and then had 14 years in Phoenix, the longest tenure of any Suns coach. He won more games than any coach of the Suns. He was the first to take the team to the NBA Finals. But he was here back in the 1970s. Today's fan probably does not recognize John MacLeod, and because of that, I would say he probably is the most underrated.

Going back a few years, I'd say Jerry Sloan was the most underrated coach in the league. He did a great job year after year, but he was in Utah and, with a market that size, he didn't get the recognition. Now he just went into the Basketball Hall of Fame, and everybody knows the great job Jerry has done. He's been with that team longer than any active coach in any sport.

The old Chicago Stadium was one of my favorite arenas. It had such a history. You used to hear heavyweight championship bouts there, Stanley Cup Finals, and lots of basketball. The three big arenas would be Chicago Stadium, old Boston Garden, and New York's Madison Square Garden—just because of the sports history that took place in those buildings. To go from growing up on a farm just outside of Williams, Iowa, sitting on the fence posts, pretending to be broadcasting sporting events for the pigs and the cattle, to walking into New York's Madison Square Garden, old Boston Garden, or old Chicago Stadium was a pretty big thrill.

Musicians are quite a crew. They're almost like pro athletes. You meet a musician, work with them, and still know them years later. When I was going to Drake University, I was playing with a lot of bands and groups. I happened to be playing with a trio in a club called Johnnie Critelli's in Des Moines, Iowa. He used to bring in some big-name musicians who might be working in Chicago and have a day or night off. He'd bring them in for a one-night stand. One night when I was working there, he brought in the great jazz trumpeter Roy Eldridge, who'd been with the Gene Krupa Band and also on his own.

Many years later, I'm doing the Phoenix Suns games, and we're going to New York to play the Knicks. John MacLeod was the head coach, and Al Bianchi was his assistant. It was a night off, and we were riding our bus to the hotel. We went down 52nd Street and drove by a place called Eddie Condon's Bar & Restaurant. I saw on the marquee, "Appearing: Little Jazz, Roy Eldridge." I said, "Boys, we've got to come back and listen to this guy." They asked me how I knew him. Many years ago, when I was in college, I worked a night with this guy. But do I really know him? No.

They wanted to watch a game that night, so it was about 10:30 or 11:00 p.m. before we went down to Eddie Condor's, a famous jazz place in New York City. We walked in, and there were not a lot of people in there. The band was taking a break and there was an intermission piano player playing up on the stage. The three of us, Al Bianchi, John MacLeod, and I, got a table near the band-stand. As we looked up, I recognized the piano player. He was a guy from Des Moines, Iowa, named Ellsworth Brown, although I later found out he was using another name.

I said to these guys, "That guy's from Des Moines." They started to laugh. When he finished playing the tune, Bianchi called up to him, "Excuse me. Do you know who this is?" He recognized me right away. He took his break, came down and sat at our table, and told me he'd been in New York for a number of years. It was about time for Roy Eldridge to go on. He was up in years by then, and he came out from the back. I recall he had slippers on and had his horn under his arm. This piano player, Ellsworth Brown, called him and said, "Look. Come over here." Roy Eldridge makes his way over to our table, and Ellsworth points at me and asks him, "Do you know this guy here?" Roy Eldridge, the great jazz player, looked at me and said, "You're that little piano man from Des Moines." Musicians, like athletes, never forget each other....

Connie Hawkins was playing with the Phoenix Suns, and the team, maybe for the first time, was on national TV. Midway through the game, Connie Hawkins drives to the basket, gets bumped, and goes down to the floor like he's never going to get up. He's flat on his back, writhing around in pain. Our trainer, Joe Proski, runs out on the floor as the play was stopped to see if Hawk is okay. Proski leans down over Hawk, and Connie looks up and says, "Hey, Prosk, your friends in Green Bay are loving it now because you're a star on national TV." Hawk gets up and walks back to the bench....

Early in my career, when I was responsible for both radio and TV, and we didn't travel with producers or directors, I hired a lot of people on the road and got to work with them a great deal. One of them was Lonnie Dale, who was in Kansas City doing some local television directing. We had just switched from Channel 12 to Channel 15 in Phoenix. Channel 12 would never send a director. I talked with our people and told them we needed a director. They asked me if I had anybody in mind, and I told them I had always liked Lonnie Dale. He had worked with me several times when I'd gone into Kansas City. Lonnie directed our games for several years. He's now one of the top directors at Turner Sports. He was the first full-time director I had for TV with the Suns.

I've worked with the same radio engineers for years. The only NBA team that takes an engineer with them on the road is the Denver Nuggets. All of the other teams, including the Suns, hire local talent. Around the league, I've had a lot of the same guys working with me year after year. In New York, Carl Infantino and his son Mike have done our games for years. In Philadelphia, Tom Keegan has been my regular engineer. In Dallas it's Jerry Ernest; in Atlanta, it's John Kramer; in Minneapolis, it's Wayne Selly; in

Houston, Mickey Hicks; in San Antonio, Lou Houck; and in L.A., Tony Noto. All of them are real pros and great to work with.

The only bad situation I had with an engineer was at Boston Garden when I came into the league. They had an engineer there who was a terrific guy and happened to be the secretary of the union, but he retired. His replacement was also head of the union, and he would show up, set up the equipment, and sit there eating popcorn and peanuts and drinking beer. If he got a call from the station telling him we needed more broadcast balance, he wouldn't do anything. I wasn't a big fan of his.

One year, I go in to do the game and make my way to my position. There's no equipment—nothing. I had the engineer's home number, so I called him. He said, "I wasn't booked to do this game." I said, "You were. I've got your name; I've got your confirmation." "Well, I didn't think I was doing it. I'm not coming in there now." I told him, "Don't ever show up again when I'm in town." I had some apparatus with me I could hook into the telephone to do the game. That's the only time I can recall when the engineer didn't show....

I have a lot of speaking engagements, and I was asked at one recently if any of the Phoenix Suns players ever smoke. I had to laugh because, going back 30 years, if you walked into a locker room, even at halftime, there might be some guys lighting up. How about baseball? You could look down at the dugout and see guys down there smoking. They finally made them go down in the runway out of sight. I can safely say that in the NBA now, I don't think you'll find any cigarette smoking. But back in those days, it happened.

Everybody in the NBA will tell you that a good trade is one that helps both teams. Sometimes it works out that way and sometimes it doesn't. Over the last 10 years, trades in the NBA are made for different reasons than they used to be. Going back 20 to 30 years, trades were made more to improve teams and to obtain certain types of players. Now, a lot of trades are made because of contract situations or what the salary involvement is. With the salary cap and luxury tax, trades today are made for reasons beyond what a straight player-to-player trade might be. Any time you make a trade, it's a gamble. If it works well for both teams, then it's been successful. It's interesting because if you trade a player that the fans love, it hurts for a while. That's happened to the Suns with players like Jeff Hornacek, Larry Nance, and Dan Majerle. It takes a while for the Suns to get over that because in a medium-sized NBA market like Phoenix, it's easy for fans to get attached to a player. Once they're traded, those fans may not be happy. Trades don't always work out the way you want them to.

We've had a lot of players that were great in the community. I say that in an affectionate way to the ownership that's been involved since day one and still today. Jerry Colangelo said, "It's not what the community can do for you, it's what you can do for the community that important." That's always been one of the strong points of the Suns' organization; their players give back to the community. That started on day one of the franchise and continues to this day. Suns Charities is a viable organization that contributes over a million dollars each year to local charities. The NBA is also very involved in getting the players active in their communities. It's obvious that today's players, with the salaries they make, are vitally concerned with giving back to the community. Through the years, the Suns would have to be number one in that category. It's important for the players to do it, and I'm very proud of the fact that over the years virtually all of our players have never hesitated to be part of giving back to the community.

Many times people are shocked when I tell them the first NBA basketball game I ever saw was in Iowa—Waterloo, Iowa. People will always challenge me on that. I tell them to go look it up, as we say. In 1946, Waterloo, Iowa was in the NBA. The team was originally supposed to be in Des Moines, but they had problems trying to get an arena so it moved to Waterloo where they had an arena called the Hippodrome. That's where they played in 1946, and was the first game I saw—the Waterloo Hawks and the Tri-City Blackhawks. Tri-City is now better known as the Quad Cities. Tri-Cities played in Moline, Illinois and, a few years later, was coached by Red Auerbach. The Tri-City team eventually went to Milwaukee and then to St. Louis and then to Atlanta. That was the first NBA game I saw and saw several more there. Years later, I was talking with George Mikan, the great, great center, at one of our games in Minnesota. I told him, "You know the first time I saw you play was in Waterloo, Iowa." He laughed and said, "Oh yes, I remember the Hippodrome." So the first NBA game I got to see was in 1946 when I was in high school.

Babe Bisignano became a great friend. He had owned a restaurant and bar in Des Moines, Iowa, forever. Anybody who has ever been in Des Moines has been to Babe's. When I was in college, I went there. Later on, I got to know Babe. Now, moving ahead to when I'm with the Suns, Babe has a daughter, who is a nun in Tucson. She has a school there. I'd get her some tickets, and some of the sisters would come up to Suns' games.

When I was back in Des Moines, I would always go see Babe. One time, a number of years ago, I'm back there staying at the Savery Hotel. I knew that his wife had recently passed away, and he'd been hit pretty hard. I went out to dinner with some friends on a Saturday night and was back at the hotel about 11:30 p.m.

Babe's restaurant was just around the corner from the Savery Hotel. I decided to walk over there to say "Hi" to him. It was midnight, almost closing time. Babe had a big booth in the back, and he was always sitting there with judges and lawyers and influential people. When I walked in, he was there with a crowd of people so I didn't want to bother him. I sat down at the bar and ordered a beer. In a few minutes, those people started to leave because it was closing time.

Babe spotted me, and he called out, "Al, why didn't you come over? How long have you been here?" He said, "Just a minute, I'll be right back." He was getting these other people. The bartender came over and told me that this was the first time he had been back to the restaurant talking to people since his wife passed away. Pretty soon Babe came over and sat down to talk.

He asked me when the last time I'd had his pizza was. I said, "Well, it's been a while." He said, "Okay, you're having it tonight. Lock the front door." He keeps the bartender and a waitress on. They fire up the oven, and he started making pizza. The first pizza comes out, and there's a knock on the door. Babe gets up and says, "Oh, that's the guy from the newspaper." So he lets in this man, Chuck Offenberger, a columnist for the newspaper.

Babe says to me, "Have you read my book?" I said, "No." He told the bartender to call a cab. About 20 minutes go by, the cabdriver comes to the door, and we let him in. Babe said to him, "Okay, here's 50 bucks. Go to City Drug; they have my book there. Go get a copy and bring back the change." Half an hour later, here comes the guy with the book. Babe autographed it, "Al McCoy— I knew you, kid, when you came in here with a fake ID." He was always a good guy, and he was Mr. Des Moines for a long, long time. Rocky Marciano was killed in a private plane crash near Des Moines. Rocky was on his way to his own birthday party, being thrown for him by Babe.

At one time, we were doing a live wrestling television show in the studios of Channel 12 in Phoenix on a Saturday afternoon. It was an hour-long show. It was done to promote the wrestling card that night at the Coliseum. I was the play-by-play announcer as well as the host on the Wrestling TV Hour. My analyst was a former wrestler, an old-timer who shall remain nameless.

They always brought in enough of a crowd to make it look good on TV. They might have had 40 people sitting ringside. But wrestling fans are always enthusiastic no matter the number. These two wrestlers—One of them was "Sputnik Monroe." In one of the matches we had on TV, "Sputnik" took something out from his trunks, some kind of a small knife or a razor blade. As he struck his opponent, he cut him on the forehead. It's an old wrestlers' trick they'd use many times to get the crowd fired up. Well, it worked. The blood started gushing right away and the fans were going bananas. We had a camera set up on a pedestal above the ring. The minute that blood started flowing from the forehead of this wrestler, the young man who was on that camera fainted and fell off the pedestal and down onto the mat. At the same time, some fans started to jump into the ring. The former wrestler who was working with me shouted, "Al! Al! The kid just died! The kid is dead! He fell off the camera!" The place is going bananas. I'm trying to calm him down and make some semblance of all of this. It goes on for several minutes and all of a sudden we're hearing sirens. The big studio door at the back of Channel 12 opens up and police come pouring in. We hurriedly sign off the air. The police ushered everyone out. I went into the dressing room afterward and said to the promoter, "Mike, this is unbelievable." He said, "What do you mean? There was nothing wrong with that." I said, "I don't think you'll ever be on Channel 12 again." And they were not.

When I found out I was going to be a bobblehead, they took some pictures of me so they could manufacture it. I didn't think too much about it. The night they were going to unveil it and give it away at the arena, they had a luncheon for me. Robert Sarver, our owner, who has a sense of humor, was introducing me at the luncheon. He held up one of the bobbleheads and said, "Here it is. The Suns have had bobbleheads before, but this is the first time that we've had a life-size bobblehead." I told him, "Robert, I'll do the jokes, if you don't mind." The interesting thing was, and I say this tongue-in-cheek, they had more reaction to my bobblehead than they had for any of the players. It was being sold on eBay for a long time. I still have people approach me with them, and I'll always autograph them.

A couple of years ago, the Chicago Cubs were in town to play the Arizona Diamondbacks. I usually go over to see some of the Cubs and the announcers and others I know. Bob Brenly, the one-time skipper of the Diamondbacks, now is the color analyst on Chicago Cubs television. When I walked in the press room before the game, he spotted me and came over. We visited for a few minutes. He said, "Al, there's somebody here who really wants to say hello to you." I said, "Oh, great." He took me over to a table and Len Kasper, who had just taken the job a couple of years before as the WGN-TV play-by-play announcer was there. We shook hands and talked for a minute. Finally Len said to me, "We've met before." I said, "Really." He said, "Yes, I went to Central Michigan University. When the Suns drafted Dan Majerle, who went to Central Michigan, the Suns played a preseason game there. I said, "Yeah, I remember that." He said, "Do you remember the young guy who helped you set up your broadcasting equipment?" I chuckled. He said, "That was me. I have to tell you that you were so gracious. You talked about broadcasting. You really gave me help and were an inspiration in my continuing on in my TV career." He's had a great career and is a very outstanding young broadcaster. It was great to hear his comments.

I still love going back to my home in Williams, Iowa. Whenever I go back, that's when all these things come back to mind. Where did the years go? They've gone by in a hurry. It seems like yesterday I was at KJFJ in Webster City, Iowa, and had a room there for five bucks a week. I wonder if that room is still available.

Here's an example of why I'm proud to be an Iowan: After my mother had passed away, my dad was living in an apartment in a retirement community in Webster City, Iowa. He fell. Fortunately he didn't break any bones, but he was taken to a hospital, and I was notified. I happened to be on the road with the Suns in New Jersey. It was just before the All-Star break. I was able to fly back to Iowa and rent a car and get to Webster City to visit my dad. I was having to work to get him to someplace to recuperate. Although he had no broken bones, he was a little shaken with the fall and his age. After I seen him at the hospital, I went to his apartment to get his mail so I could go through it and take care of anything that need attention.

I was staying at the Norseman's Inn in Williams, Iowa. This was in January, and there was snow all over the place, as it happens in Iowa, and the temperature was down near zero. I got to my motel and parked the rental car and went into my room. I put down the mail, took off my coat and realized I couldn't find the car keys. What had happened to my car keys? They had been, inadvertently, by me, locked in the car. What am I going to do? I go back out and look and, sure enough, I can see them in the ignition...but the doors are locked. There was a small bar in this motel so I went in there. Some truck drivers were in there and they came out and took a look at it. They took a hanger but couldn't get it unlocked. They mentioned that across the highway was another motel and restaurant and garage and there might be someone there.

Now, this was on a Saturday night at ten o'clock. I bundled up and walked across the road. Just as I got there, the one mechanic they had on duty was just leaving. I told him my problem. He had me jump in his pickup, and he took me back to the car. He attempted to get into the car while I held a flashlight for him. It was close to zero, and we were freezing. He could not get inside the car doors to open it. Finally he decided the only way he could do it was to bend part of the top of the door out. I told him to go ahead and do it. So, after standing there holding the flashlight for him for about 45 minutes and freezing, he got down inside and got the door open, and I got the car keys.

I can't tell you what a sigh of relief because I was a long way from Des Moines where the car had been rented, and I just didn't know what I would have done if I hadn't been able to get the keys out. As he was putting his tools away, I said, "I can't thank you enough. I really appreciate this. What do I owe you for the job?" He looked at me and said, "You don't owe me anything." I said, "What do you mean?" He said, "You don't owe me anything." I said, "I've got to give you something." He said, "No. I'll tell you what. Somewhere down the line, you may have an opportunity to help somebody out. When you do, you can just think of someone who helped you out one time." I tell the story and still get tears in my eyes.

But, that's not the end of the story. I thanked him again. We shook hands. He got in his pickup and drove off on that cold Saturday night in Iowa. About five years later, I'm on a talk show on WHO radio, Des Moines, Iowa, with my long-time friend, Jim Zabel. I am in Phoenix talking on the phone. People are calling in asking about the Suns and the NBA. A call comes in, and the gentleman says, "Al McCoy, I don't know if you'll remember me, but four or five years ago you locked your keys in the car at the Norseman's Inn in Williams. I'm the guy who got the door open." I had to tell the whole story again. It was fantastic. Only in Iowa. Every time I tell this story, I think of the great line in the motion picture *Field of Dreams*, "Is this heaven? No. It's Iowa."

Sports were always big in the Midwest. I can go back to Williams, Iowa, walk into the local bar and grill or drugstore, and they will know everything about the Phoenix Suns—when they played, who they beat, who their leading scorer is, and who's atop the division. Sports are such a big part of their daily lives. I don't know whether you just grow up that way or not. It was true when I was a kid and—I'll tell you what—it's still true today.

I'm very pleased that both my mother and father got to spend time with me when I was with the Phoenix Suns. My mother passed away in 1995; my father in 2000. My father was 98 and my mother 95. They were great basketball fans, both when I was playing in high school and later doing broadcasting. They had wintered in Phoenix for many years.

My mom would get so excited at some of the games; she'd really get on the officials. I had to tell my wife, "You've got to tell her I'm not going to let her come to these games if she doesn't calm down." I'm very happy that my mother and father, who were hard-working farm people from Iowa, were able to realize the success I've had. They watched on TV, heard me on radio, and went to a lot of Suns games on top of that....

By the way, I forgot to tell you how I found out I had been voted into the Basketball Hall of Fame. That summer I came into my office one day and had a message from John D. Oleva, who is president of the Basketball Hall of Fame in Springfield, Massachusetts. I thought, "I don't know what he wants with me," so I didn't return the call. A couple of days later, I was in the office. Again, I got a message from John D. Oleva. I thought he was probably wanting some information about a former player or former coach so decided I'd better get back to him. So, two days later I called him and said, "This is Al McCoy, out in Phoenix. What can I do for you?" He said, "Well, you can't do anything for me. I think I have something to pass along to you that maybe you'll be very proud of. You have been selected as the 18th Broadcaster to receive the Curt Gowdy Award in the Basketball Hall of Fame. Obviously it was mindboggling, to say the least. It was a tremendous surprise.

I went back to Springfield, Massachusetts in September to be there for the Hall of Fame weekend and receive the honor for the electronic media Curt Gowdy Basketball Hall of Fame, which was terrific. My whole family was there. My good friend, Greg Schulte, was there as well as Joe Proski and some other friends. It was really the highlight of my career. I had always felt the two premiere NBA basketball broadcasters were Marty Glickman, of the New York Knicks, and my long-time friend, Chick Hearn, of the Los Angeles Lakers. In my acceptance speech, I mentioned that to be considered in the same Hall of Fame with those two was just fantastic.

Also, my original sidekick, color announcer, Rod Hundley was also in that list so it certainly made it outstanding.

I mentioned, in my acceptance speech three people who certainly were dominant in my receiving this. My first high school basketball coach, Chuck Lovin, who taught me that winning is a lot more fun than losing. To my college professor, Professor Jim Duncan, Drake University, who prepared me for the real world of broadcasting. And, of course, to Jerry Colangelo, the former owner-president of the Phoenix Suns, who gave me the opportunity to be the voice of the Suns. That was tremendous to receive that honor and to be honored by the Basketball Hall of Fame.

Well, I guess we are up-to-date.

After making the NBA finals on two occasions, the Suns are still aiming for that NBA Championship and I'm still hoping for a "ring." As I look back on the years, it has been a "great ride" and I am expecting a lot more to come.

It has been great to have been a part of the big band era...those days when radio was king and the early days of TV...black and white and a little "snowy."

I have always been proud of growing up on a farm in Iowa. I wouldn't give anything for that experience. But, now I am a long-time Arizonan and proud of that.

I have been truly blessed with a wonderful, supportive family and a 38-year career with the Phoenix Suns.

But...OH BROTHER!! I'll have more to write someday, however I am sure there is a game tonight and I will be courtside...microphone in hand...ready to describe another exciting game with the Phoenix Suns...I hope you will be tuned in!

Shazam!

Al McCoy

THE REAL MCCOY

New York AP

The phrase "The Real McCoy" is said to have originated in the early 1900s when a man claiming to be Al McCoy, a boxing champion, mooched drinks along New York's Broadway. One day the fighter met up with the imposter in a bar and after identifying himself, flattened him with one punch. The bartender is reported to have remarked "That guy must be the real McCoy."

OTHER BOOKS BY RICH WOLFE

Da Coach (Mike Ditka)
I Remember Harry Caray
There's No Expiration Date on Dreams (Tom Brady)
He Graduated Life with Honors and No Regrets (Pat Tillman)
Take This Job and Love It (Jon Gruden)
Been There, Shoulda Done That (John Daly)
Oh, What a Knight (Bob Knight)
And the Last Shall Be First (Kurt Warner)
Remembering Jack Buck
Sports Fans Who Made Headlines
Fandemonium
Remembering Dale Earnhardt
I Saw It On the Radio (Vin Scully)
Outta Here—(Harry Kalas)
Tim Russert, We Heartily Knew Ye

For Yankee Fans Only
For Cubs Fans Only
For Red Sox Fans Only
For Cardinals Fans Only
For Packers Fans Only
For Hawkeye Fans Only
For Browns Fans Only
For Mets Fans Only
For Notre Dame Fans Only—
  The New Saturday Bible
For Bronco Fans Only
For Nebraska Fans Only

For Buckeye Fans Only
For Georgia Bulldog Fans Only
For South Carolina Fans Only
For Clemson Fans Only
For Cubs Fans Only—Volume II
For Oklahoma Fans Only
For Yankee Fans Only—Volume II
For Mizzou Fans Only
For Kansas City Chiefs Fans Only
For K-State Fans Only
For KU Fans Only (Kansas)

All books are the same size, format and price.
Questions? Contact the author directly at 602-738-5889.

Now let's meet "The Man In The Middle"
for Williams High School, Allen McCoy